Collins English Readers

Amazing Architects and Artists

Level 2
CEF A2–B1

RPL BOOK SALE
NON-REFUNDABLE

Text by
F.H. Cornish

Series edited by
Fiona MacKenzie

Collins

HarperCollins Publishers
77–85 Fulham Palace Road
Hammersmith London W6 8JB

10 9 8 7 6 5 4 3 2 1

Original text
© The Amazing People Club Ltd

Adapted text
© HarperCollins Publishers Ltd 2014

ISBN: 978-0-00-754496-7

Collins® is a registered trademark of
HarperCollins Publishers Limited

www.collinselt.com

A catalogue record for this book is available
from the British Library

Printed in the UK by Martins the Printers

All rights reserved. No part of this book
may be reproduced, stored in a retrieval
system, or transmitted in any form or
by any means, electronic, mechanical,
photocopying, recording or otherwise,
without the prior permission in writing
of the Publisher. This book is sold subject
to the conditions that it shall not, by way
of trade or otherwise, be lent, re-sold,
hired out or otherwise circulated without
the Publisher's prior consent in any form
of binding or cover other than that in
which it is published and without a similar
condition including this condition being
imposed on the subsequent purchaser.

HarperCollins does not warrant that
www.collinselt.com or any other website
mentioned in this title will be provided
uninterrupted, that any website will be
error free, that defects will be corrected, or
that the website or the server that makes it
available are free of viruses or bugs. For full
terms and conditions please refer to the site
terms provided on the website.

These readers are based on original texts
(BioViews®) published by The Amazing
People Club group.® BioViews® and The
Amazing People Club® are registered
trademarks and represent the views of the
author.

BioViews® are scripted virtual interview
based on research about a person's life and
times. As in any story, the words are only
an interpretation of what the individuals
mentioned in the BioViews® could have
said. Although the interpretations are
based on available research, they do not
purport to represent the actual views of
the people mentioned. The interpretations
are made in good faith, recognizing
that other interpretations could also be
made. The author and publisher disclaim
any responsibility from any action that
readers take regarding the BioViews® for
educational or other purposes. Any use
of the BioViews® materials is the sole
responsibility of the reader and should
be supported by their own independent
research.

Cover image © Aleksandra Kovac/
Shutterstock

MIX
Paper from
responsible sources
FSC C007454
www.fsc.org

FSC™ is a non-profit international organisation established to promote the
responsible management of the world's forests. Products carrying the FSC
label are independently certified to assure consumers that they come from
forests that are managed to meet the social, economic and ecological needs
of present and future generations, and other controlled sources.

Find out more about HarperCollins and the environment at
www.harpercollins.co.uk/green

✦ CONTENTS ✦

Collins Amazing People Readers are collections of short stories. Each book presents the life story of five or six people whose lives and achievements have made a difference to our world today. The stories are carefully graded to ensure that you, the reader, will both enjoy and benefit from your reading experience.

You can choose to enjoy the book from start to finish or to dip in to your favourite story straight away. Each story is entirely independent.

After every story a short timeline brings together the most important events in each person's life into one short report. The timeline is a useful tool for revision purposes.

Words which are above the required reading level are underlined the first time they appear in each story. All underlined words are defined in the glossary at the back of the book. Levels 1 and 2 take their definitions from the *Collins COBUILD Essential English Dictionary* and levels 3 and 4 from the *Collins COBUILD Advanced English Dictionary*.

To support both teachers and learners, additional materials are available online at www.collinselt.com/readers.

The Amazing People Club®

Collins Amazing People Readers are adaptations of original texts published by The Amazing People Club. The Amazing People Club is an educational publishing house. It was founded in 2006 by educational psychologist and management leader Dr Charles Margerison and publishes books, eBooks, audio books, iBooks and video content which bring readers 'face to face' with many of the world's most inspiring and influential characters from the fields of art, science, music, politics, medicine and business.

◆ THE GRADING SCHEME ◆

The Collins COBUILD Grading Scheme has been created using the most up-to-date language usage information available today. Each level is guided by a brand new comprehensive grammar and vocabulary framework, ensuring that the series will perfectly match readers' abilities.

		CEF band	Pages	Word count	Headwords
Level 1	elementary	A2	64	5,000–8,000	approx. 700
Level 2	pre-intermediate	A2–B1	80	8,000–11,000	approx. 900
Level 3	intermediate	B1	96	11,000–15,000	approx. 1,100
Level 4	upper intermediate	B2	112	15,000–18,000	approx. 1,700

For more information on the Collins COBUILD Grading Scheme, including a full list of the grammar structures found at each level, go to www.collinselt.com/readers/gradingscheme.

Also available online: Make sure that you are reading at the right level by checking your level on our website (www.collinselt.com/readers/levelcheck).

Leonardo da Vinci

• ◆ •

1452–1519

the man who painted the *Mona Lisa*

I had many careers during my life. I was a painter, an architect, an engineer and a scientist. But I was also a <u>dreamer</u> who <u>dreamed</u> of the future. Some of the things I dreamed about only happened many years after my death.

◆ ◆ ◆

I was born, on 15th April 1452, in a village near the Italian town of Vinci. In those days, all the great cities of Italy were separate countries. Vinci belonged to the city of Florence.

My father, Piero Fruosino di Antonio da Vinci, was a lawyer in Florence. My mother, who was called Caterina, was a poor girl from the village. My father gave me a good education, and perhaps he wanted me to become a lawyer like him. However, my interest was in art.

When I was 14, I became an <u>apprentice</u> of the artist Andrea del Verrocchio. I worked with him for ten years while he taught me. He taught me the arts of painting and drawing as well as <u>metalwork</u> and other arts. Soon, I began to help my teacher with his paintings.

I was a good student, and by the age of 20, I was a member of a group of people called the Guild of Saint Luke. Some of the people in this group were artists, but others were doctors. The <u>detailed</u> drawings that artists made of parts of the human body – anatomical drawings – were important for doctors. So the two groups of people spent time together.

I enjoyed making these scientific drawings. But I also made <u>religious</u> pictures. My <u>patrons</u> always wanted these, and I was good at drawing and painting people. I could easily draw things that were in front of me, like many other artists. But I could also draw things that didn't exist. Having this skill made me an <u>inventor</u> as well as an artist. All my life, I used my imagination, as well as my eyes and hands. I used them all to invent things, as well as to make pictures.

◆ ◆ ◆

In 1481, the <u>monks</u> at Scopeto <u>commissioned</u> me to make a picture for them. I started work on the painting, which was called *The Adoration of the Magi*. But I didn't finish the job. I had to leave Florence suddenly. Why was this? I'd made a musical <u>instrument</u> from silver. It was a kind of <u>harp</u> which looked like a horse's head. A prince called Lorenzo de' Medici heard about this instrument. Lorenzo was the ruler of the city at that time. He decided to send me to Milan with the instrument. He wanted to give it to his enemy, Ludovico Sforza, the ruler of Milan. He wanted Florence to <u>make peace with</u> Milan and he hoped that his present could help this to happen.

I did what Lorenzo wanted me to do, and for the next 17 years I spent most of my time working in Milan. It was there in 1483, that I made the first of my two paintings of *The Virgin of the Rocks*. Two years later, I painted *The Lady with an Ermine*. These paintings later became very famous. I also designed a kind of <u>parachute</u> at that time.

In 1487, I made a drawing which is also very famous. I was very interested in <u>proportions</u> at that time. And I was interested in the work of Vitruvius. This ancient Roman architect had written a lot about the subject. He thought that there were rules about proportions in nature. And he thought that there were similar rules for the proportions between the different parts of buildings. I agreed with him. My drawing, which is now called *The Vitruvian Man*, shows a man's body. The arms and legs of the man are drawn in two different positions. And the man is contained by both a circle and a square. I thought that the proportions between the parts of a human body were interesting. I thought that they were like the proportions

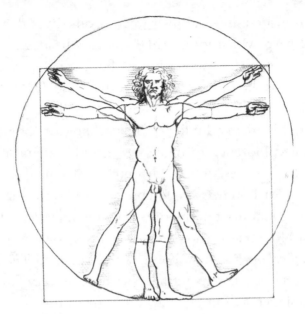

Leonardo da Vinci's *Vitruvian Man*

in art and architecture and in the rest of nature. I wrote my thoughts about this subject next to my drawing.

Those years in Milan were very busy for me, and I worked on the <u>cathedral</u> in the city, as well as on paintings for rich patrons. I also made a <u>ceramic</u> model of a horse, called the *Gran Cavallo*. My idea was to make a very large copy of this model, using the metal called bronze. It didn't happen – the bronze <u>version</u> was never made. Why? Unfortunately, the government of the city used the bronze to make large guns. They needed guns to defend Milan from its enemies.

While I was in Milan, I heard from my mother. Her health wasn't good. She came to live with me in 1493, and she died two years later. I went on with my work. Between 1495 and 1498, I created a large <u>mural</u> in a church. The painting was called *The Last Supper*. But Milan was no longer a safe place, and in 1499, a French army, led by King Louis the Twelfth, <u>invaded</u> the city. I didn't stay to fight. I was 48 years old and I wasn't well. I couldn't fight.

◆ ◆ ◆

I left Milan and I went to live in Venice. I was too old for fighting, but I could design buildings and machines for defence against enemies. The people of Venice soon asked me to design defences for their beautiful city. So I became a <u>military</u> architect and engineer for a year. But after I finished that work, I didn't want to stay in Venice. I decided to move back to my home city, Florence.

I enjoyed being in Florence again. I lived in a <u>monastery</u>, so I was able to paint in the monks' <u>workshop</u>. I used it as my <u>studio</u>. And there were so many beautiful buildings in the city! I loved walking through the streets and looking at the <u>details</u> of the architecture. But I also enjoyed looking at the natural world. I looked especially at the birds. They sang happily and flew happily through the air. 'If *they* can fly, why can't I do that?' I asked myself. 'Why can't men and women fly too?'

That question stayed in my mind, and I made some quick drawings – some sketches. I wanted to invent a flying machine. So I made sketches of flying machines that had moving wings. They *were* only sketches. 'But one day,' I told myself, 'people *will* be able to fly.'

I dreamed of flying, but all around me people were talking about war. In 1502, Cesare Borgia, the city's new leader, asked me to work for him. I designed <u>weapons</u> for him, and military buildings. In those days, I had to spend a lot of time travelling. There were long journeys on bad roads. These journeys were very tiring. Between my travels I tried to paint, but it was difficult to finish many pictures. In 1506, I decided to return again to Milan.

Milan was now a safe place for me, and I had a lot of work to do there. It included many different projects, from church paintings to military designs. I often had to <u>interrupt</u> my artistic work while I did other jobs. Sometimes these <u>interruptions</u> were very long. For example, in 1503, I started painting the *Mona Lisa*, my most famous <u>portrait,</u> but I wasn't able to complete it until 1519. During this time, I *was* able to return to my medical studies. In 1510 and 1511, I cut up dead bodies and made detailed anatomical drawings of parts of them. I completed over 200 of these.

During my life, I made about 2,500 drawings of different kinds. It's a strange fact that very many of these still exist, but fewer than twenty of my paintings can still be seen. Why is this? Have bad people destroyed them? No, they've disappeared and it was my fault. I often made experiments with new kinds of paint. Some of my new paints weren't very good. Many of my paintings destroyed *themselves*, because of my bad paints.

◆ ◆ ◆

In 1513, I moved again. This time, I moved to Rome. The <u>pope</u> asked me to work for him there, and I lived in Rome until 1516. Two famous artists, Raphael and Michelangelo, were also there at the time. We all worked on art projects for churches in the city. This work was interesting, but I had other plans too. I wanted to save people's lives. I wanted to cut up dead bodies and to study them. I believed that this kind of science – pathology – could help living people. But the pope didn't agree with me. When he ordered me to stop my medical studies, I decided to leave Rome.

I returned once more to Milan, which the French king, Francis the First, now ruled. I met him and I liked him. Francis was a clever young man with the mind of an artist and we had conversations about many things. He offered me a house in Amboise, in the Loire region of France. The house was near his castle. Francis said that he wanted to learn from me. I accepted his offer and I made the long journey across France. It was a good thing to do. In France, I was given everything that I needed for my work. Most days, the king walked to my house. We discussed my scientific ideas and sometimes we discussed the king's political problems too. I stayed in France until my death on 2nd May 1519.

I spent much of my time in France writing notes about my ideas. I wanted the scientists of the future to have them. But I made these notes in back-to-front writing, so that no one who came to my house could easily read them. I didn't want anyone to steal my work while I was alive. In fact, people weren't able to read these notes until 1651, when they were finally printed in a book. That was over 130 years after my death!

In my notes, I wrote about my work and my life. During my life, I invented new ways of thinking. During my life, I asked new questions about our world and its people. During my life, I studied art, anatomy, architecture, <u>geometry</u>, <u>geology</u>, mathematics, and pathology. And I hoped for a better future.

The Life of Leonardo da Vinci

1452   Leonardo di ser Piero da Vinci was born in the village of Anchiano, near the town of Vinci in Italy.

1467   At the age of 14, he became the apprentice of the artist, Andrea del Verrocchio, in Florence.

1472   Leonardo became a member of the Painters' Guild of Florence.

*c.*1472–1475   He painted *The Annunciation*.

*c.*1474–1478   He painted a portrait of Ginevra de' Benci.

1478   He painted *The Benois Madonna* (*The Madonna with Flowers*).

1478–1480   He painted *The Madonna of the Carnation* (*The Madonna with Child*).

1480   He painted *Saint Jerome in the Wilderness*.

1481   Leonardo began work on *The Adoration of the Magi*, for the monastery of San Donato at Scopeto.

1482   He moved to Milan, and worked for Ludovico Sforza, as a painter and an engineer.

1483   He painted the first version of *The Virgin of the Rocks* and sketched the design for a parachute.

1485   Leonardo painted *The Lady with an Ermine*. He also sketched the designs for several military vehicles.

1487   He drew the 'Vitruvian Man' with notes, and sketched the design of a fighting ship.

1488   Leonardo designed a city of the future and sketched the designs for a flying machine.

1489–1490   He sketched the design for a kind of computer.

1492   Leonardo completed the ceramic model horse for the Francesco Sforza Monument. The bronze version was never made.

1495–1498   *The Last Supper* and the second *Madonna of the Rocks* were painted.

1499–1500   He spent time in Venice before returning to Florence. Leonardo was commissioned to paint *The Virgin and Child with Saint Anne and Saint John the Baptist*. He finished a sketch for it, but never completed the painting.

1500   Leonardo returned to Florence. He began painting *The Virgin and Child with Saint Anne* (completed in 1510). He sketched the design for a gun.

1502   He worked for Cesare Borgia, as a military architect and engineer. He sketched the design for a bridge across the Golden Horn in Constantinople (now called Istanbul), but it was never built.

1503   Leonardo began painting the famous *Mona Lisa* (completed in 1519). He was also commissioned to paint the Battle of Anghiara, on a wall in Florence's Palazzo Vecchio.

1505   He completed his notes on *The Flight of Birds*, which he'd started around 1490.

1510   Leonardo and Marcantonio della Torre wrote the *Work of Theoretical Anatomy*. Leonardo also painted *The Virgin and Child with St Anne*.

1513–1516   Leonardo lived in the Vatican, Rome.

1516–1519   The King of France asked Leonardo to work for him. Leonardo moved to Amboise, France. He lived and worked there until his death at the age of 67.

Christopher Wren

◆ ◆ ◆

1632–1723

the man who rebuilt London

When the Great Fire of London destroyed most of the city in 1666, I was given the job of rebuilding it. My largest building in the city, Saint Paul's <u>Cathedral</u>, is my <u>memorial</u>.

◆ ◆ ◆

I was born in Wiltshire, in England on 20th October 1632. My early life was difficult. My mother died when I was young, and soon after, the English <u>Civil War</u> began. This was a war between the supporters of King Charles the First and a group of people called the <u>Parliamentarians</u>. The Parliamentarians believed that the country's <u>parliament</u>, not the king, must rule the country. And they didn't like the country's religion – the Church of England. They wanted a much simpler kind of religion. The leader of these Parliamentarians was a man called Oliver Cromwell.

I was only ten years old when the Civil War began. My father and my uncle Matthew were both important leaders in the Church of England. My family were Royalists – we supported King Charles. Unfortunately, the Parlimentarians won the war and the king was <u>arrested</u>. It was a dangerous time for Royalists. My uncle Matthew was arrested too, and kept in prison for 18 years. My father and I went to live quietly with my sister and her husband, at their home near Oxford.

My sister had married a man called William Holder. He was a <u>mathematician</u>, and this was lucky for me. William helped me to understand the magic of numbers. He also taught me about astronomy – the science of the stars and the planets. I left my school when I was 14 years old, but I continued to study many kinds of science. With the help of a man called Doctor Scarborough, I made many anatomical drawings – drawings of parts of the human body.

◆ ◆ ◆

In 1649, I began to study at Wadham College, in the famous University of Oxford. That year, King Charles was finally killed by the Parliamentarians. They cut off his head in front of a large crowd of people. It was a time of great fear in the country, but I was safe in Oxford. I happily continued my scientific studies.

I stayed in Oxford after I had earned my degree, and I continued to make many scientific experiments.

I was especially interested in engineering projects and in anatomical experiments. But I also designed some measuring instruments for surveying. Surveying is the science of making the measurements that builders need to plan their buildings.

At that time, many people tried to invent a way of finding a ship's position at sea. I thought hard about that problem too. And I also worked on military building projects. I was very interested in ways of defending cities and harbours.

Several English universities noticed my work in all these subjects. In 1657, I became Professor of Astronomy at Gresham College, London. And four years later, I returned to Oxford University as Professor of Astronomy there. Although Oliver Cromwell still ruled the country, it was an exciting time for me.

In 1660, I met with some other people who were interested in science and we created the Royal Society. We wanted more people to know about science. The great scientist Sir Isaac Newton was one of our members. Why was our group a *Royal* society? It was because England had a king again. Oliver Cromwell had died, and King Charles the Second – the son of Charles the First – now ruled the country. The new king was interested in our work and in our society.

◆ ◆ ◆

For a few years, I continued with my scientific work, especially in mathematics. Then in 1663, I began a new career. My uncle, who was now a <u>bishop</u> in the Church of England, asked me to design a building. He wanted to build a <u>chapel</u> at Pembroke College in Cambridge. The college was a part of Cambridge University.

At that time, the job of professional architect didn't exist. Rich people who knew about mathematics designed their own houses. And large projects, like churches, were often designed by the workers who built them.

I thought that architecture was a science as well as an art. And I thought that science was an important part of the design of buildings. I knew about science, so I decided to make the design for the chapel at Cambridge. And at the same time I was <u>commissioned</u> to design a building for Oxford University too – the Sheldonian Theatre.

I'd seen lots of old English buildings and many of them were churches and chapels. They were all built in <u>medieval</u> styles, especially the <u>gothic</u> style. However, when I was a student, I'd read *On Architecture* by Vitruvius, the Roman architect. This famous book told me about building in the <u>classical</u> style. This style was very different from the gothic style, and it interested me very much.

In 1664, I went to Rome itself. I was able to study the Theatre of Marcellus there, which helped me with the Oxford building. And when I visited Paris the next year,

I was able to see some new French churches. They gave me lots of ideas.

♦ ◆ ♦

The Civil War had finished, but the English people still had many problems. In 1665, a terrible illness called the plague began to kill people in London. During the next year, the plague killed about one-sixth of all the people who lived in the city. London was a small, crowded city then, on the north side of the River Thames.

I didn't live in London at that time, so I wasn't in much danger. And although the London plague was a terrible disaster, it was *another* disaster in the city, in September 1666, which completely changed my life. On the second day of the month, a terrible fire started in the city. It burned for several days and it destroyed a very large number of buildings.

Most of the houses in the city were built of wood, and they burned very quickly. But many of the stone churches were destroyed too. One of these was London's huge gothic cathedral – Saint Paul's. About two-thirds of the city's buildings disappeared in those few days. This terrible event is still called the Great Fire of London.

The Great Fire was good for London's people in one way. It stopped the plague. And in another way, it was a good thing for me too. The city needed to be rebuilt and the king gave me a special job to do. I was <u>appointed</u> to be the Commissioner for Rebuilding the City of

London. I planned the city with help from several surveyors. We had to create a new London. Suddenly, I had a wonderful career as an architect. And for the rest of my life, architecture was my profession.

I designed some of the most important buildings in the new city. And I planned the building of 51 churches, and I did much of the design work myself. This was a big job. I also became the Surveyor for Saint Paul's Cathedral. I had already planned some repairs to the old cathedral before the fire. But that cathedral had gone and now I designed a new one. I designed a huge new building in the classical style, with a large dome.

Saint Paul's Cathedral in London

The work on the new Saint Paul's began in 1675. The cathedral took 35 years to build, and fortunately, I lived to see the end of the work. In fact, I lived for 12 more years, until I was 90 years old.

◆ ◆ ◆

After the Great Fire, I controlled the work on many other buildings, some of them for the royal family. For this reason, King Charles made me a knight in 1673 – I was now called *Sir* Christopher Wren. But in fact, I designed all kinds of buildings – palaces, theatres, museums, monuments, hospitals, and big houses, as well as churches. And I was a member of the English parliament, from 1685 to 1688 and from 1702 to 1705.

When I died, on 15th February 1723, I was buried in Saint Paul's Cathedral. The Latin words on my tomb end with the sentence, '*Lector, si monumentum requiris, circumspice*'. This means 'Reader, if you want to see his memorial, look around you'.

The Life of Christopher Wren

1632   Christopher Wren was born in East Knoyle in Wiltshire, England.

1634   His mother died soon after the birth of his sister, Elizabeth.

1635   Christopher's father became an important leader in the Church of England. In his early years, Christopher was taught at home.

1641   Christopher attended Westminster School until 1646.

1643   Christopher's older sister married William Holder, a mathematician. The family moved to Bletchingham in Oxfordshire.

1649   Christopher began studying mathematics at Oxford University. He got his first degree two years later.

1653   He got another degree and became a member of All Souls, another Oxford college. He made many scientific experiments.

1657   He was given the job of Professor of Astronomy at Gresham College, London. He often met with a group of scientists for discussions. They later started The Royal Society.

1660   A new king, Charles the Second, ruled England.

1661   Christopher became Savilian Professor of
        Astronomy at Oxford.

1663   Christopher was commissioned by his
        uncle, the Bishop of Ely, to build a chapel
        for Pembroke College, Cambridge. He was
        also commissioned to build the Sheldonian
        Theatre, Oxford, which included his
        first design for a dome. During that
        time, Christopher visited Paris to study
        architecture. He also visited Rome to see
        the work of Michelangelo, at Saint Peter's
        Church.

1666   The Great Fire of London destroyed
        13,000 homes and 70 churches. Christopher
        was appointed to be the Commissioner
        for Rebuilding the City of London. He
        produced a new plan for the city, which
        King Charles liked. For the next 30 years,
        Christopher worked on the design of new
        churches. He made several designs for Saint
        Paul's Cathedral.

1669   Christopher was appointed to be the
        Surveyor of Saint Paul's Cathedral and
        Surveyor General of the King's Works.
        He married Faith Coghill.

1672   Their first son, Gilbert was born, but he
        died when he was very young.

1675   Christopher's wife died soon after the birth of their second son. Christopher continued his work on Saint Paul's Cathedral. His design took 35 years to build. Christopher was also commissioned by King Charles to create a Royal Observatory – a building where scientists studied the stars.

1677   Christopher married Jane Fitzwilliam, who died three years later. They had two children.

1680   Christopher became President of The Royal Society for two years.

1682   He designed the Royal Hospital for Soldiers in Chelsea.

1696   He was appointed to be Surveyor of Greenwich Naval Hospital.

1697   Parts of Saint Paul's Cathedral were opened. The dome was finally completed by 1711.

1699   He was also appointed to be Surveyor of Westminster Abbey until his death.

1723   Christopher died aged 90.

Antoni Gaudí

◆ ◆ ◆

1852–1926

the man who built the *Sagrada Familia*

People will always remember me because of the strange and wonderful buildings I designed in Barcelona. My huge basilica there is not finished, but it is one of the world's most famous churches.

◆ ◆ ◆

I was born on 25th June 1852, in the town of Reus, in Catalonia. Catalonia is in Spain, near the border with France. My parents, Francesc and Antònia Gaudí, were people with strong <u>religious</u> <u>beliefs</u>, and they were happy to be Catalonians. I was their fifth child and my full name was Antoni Placid Guillem Gaudí i Cornet. My childhood was unusual. I couldn't walk or run easily, because I had a <u>rheumatic</u> illness. My illness was painful and there was no <u>cure</u> for it. My parents tried to help me with my problems, but I had to rest a lot.

When I was eleven years old, I was able to attend the religious school in our town. I enjoyed my studies there. I was very interested in <u>geometry</u> and I was very good at art. Soon, I realized that I wanted to become an architect.

♦ ◆ ♦

In 1868, we moved to Barcelona, the capital city of Catalonia. My father sold some of our family's land to pay for my higher education. Soon, I was able to study at the architectural college in Barcelona. I didn't win any important prizes there. In fact, I was an average student. But that didn't worry me. My great interest was in the <u>creative</u> design of buildings, and some of my teachers didn't understand that. I *was* interested in building with stone and with <u>bricks</u>. But I was also interested in the extra things that made a building special – <u>metalwork</u>, <u>woodwork</u>, painting on glass, and <u>ceramics</u>.

While I was a student, I worked for several architects in our city. The one who taught me most was called Joan Martorell. He was my best teacher, and he was also a man who knew many important people in Barcelona. We became friends, and he helped me later in my life.

When my time at the college was finished, I had to join the army, like all young men at that time. For three years from 1875, I was a soldier. But I was ill for most of my <u>military</u> service, so I was able to continue my studies. Although I was a soldier, I had a strong belief in peace. But I also had strong beliefs in two other things – the rights of working people, and the future of Catalonia. I didn't believe that the Spanish national government was listening to us. Our Catalonia needed more strong voices.

◆ ◆ ◆

When I started to design buildings, I did a lot of research. At that time, the 19th-century architects who had started to use medieval styles again interested me most. I was especially interested in their use of the gothic style. But I was also interested in Eastern design, and in the most recent kind of Spanish 'modernist' architecture. This style also used ideas from gothic architecture, but in a new way. I worked in all these styles. However, when I finally created my personal style, it was nature that inspired me. I used the shapes of plants as my models for the shapes of my buildings. People called it my 'organic' style because of these plant-shapes. My most famous works were built in this organic style.

◆ ◆ ◆

At the beginning of my career, the government of the city of Barcelona gave me a design job. Some of the streetlights on Plaça Reial in the city were designed by me. But my first big architectural project, was for the Mataró Workers' Cooperative. I designed some workers' houses, as well as a factory and some offices. The project wasn't completed, but people began to know about me. At about the same time, I designed some furniture which was shown at the Paris World Fair in 1878. There were fairs like this in several cities in the late nineteenth century. People came from all over the world to see the exhibitions which these cities arranged. In Paris that year, I met Eusebi Güell, a rich Catalonian businessman, who became a good friend and an important <u>client</u>.

◆ ◆ ◆

Soon I was busy with buildings in and around Barcelona. Many assistants with different skills worked for me. I designed many buildings in my life. But I also designed the things that surrounded them. I liked to create gardens and parks round my buildings. And I liked to use <u>local</u> kinds of stone in these parks and gardens. In that way, I could join the building to the park, and the park to the local <u>geology</u>. This part of an architect's work is called landscaping. And I believed that it was very important.

The inside of a building was as important for me as the outside. For this reason I always wanted to design the furniture which my clients put in my buildings. I believed that designing furniture was a big part of an architect's job. And I always tried to include the services – water <u>pipes</u>, gas pipes, electric <u>wires</u> – inside the walls of my building.

I won the largest project of my life because Joan Martorel was my friend. This project was the design of a huge church. This *Basílica Temple Expiatori de la Sagrada Familia* was also for Barcelona. Martorell knew that I

The *Sagrada Familia* in Barcelona

was the right person for this job and he told the basilica's
<u>patrons</u> about me. In 1883, I was asked to be the architect.
I started work at once on this project, which was going to
be the centre of my life for as long as I lived.

For 43 years, I worked on the church of the Sagrada
Familia. For most of that time, it wasn't the *whole* of my
life. I continued to work on many other architectural
projects as well. My most important clients for these were
Eusebi Güell and his family. They <u>commissioned</u> many
buildings and designs from me. But there were lots of
other clients too.

In those years, I designed a large number of important
buildings. Some of the most famous of these are the *Palau
Güell*, the <u>Bishops'</u> Palace in Astorga, the *Casa Milà*, and
the *Casa de los Botines*, in Léon. The *Casa de los Botines* was a
huge building with shops and offices, and apartments above
them. And in 1888, I had a <u>commission</u> which allowed
more people from outside Spain to see my work. In that
year, there was a World Fair in Barcelona. My job was to
design the Transatlantic Company's building for the Fair.

In the same year, work had begun on the *Colònia Güell*.
This was a large project outside Barcelona. It included a
factory, with workers' houses. Several different architects
designed parts of the project. After the factory and houses
were finished, Eusebi Güell commissioned a design for a
church from me. Building started, but the work was slow.
Unfortunately, the church was never completed. In 1918,
Eusebi died and his sons stopped the building work.

I worked on many small projects as well as my big jobs. I could do this because I had a large team of assistants. I continued to work for private clients and companies, as well as for the Roman Catholic Church. I enjoyed working on these projects. But by 1910, all of my time was spent on the Sagrada Familia.

Barcelona already had a <u>cathedral</u>. This new building – the Church of the Holy Family – was different. It was for the religious people of the city, but also for all religious people everywhere. In fact, I wanted it to be a church for people without religious beliefs too. It had to be a building that tourists could come to look at. It had to be a building that its patrons could love.

Soon, the basilica became my second home. Some people said that it was my *first* home. In fact, in the last year of my life I lived in a <u>studio</u> on the site of the church. People often said that the work on the basilica was taking a very long time. 'My client is not in a hurry,' I replied. I meant that God was my client.

My beliefs gave me a strong wish to continue with the work, year after year. The design was very complicated. There were towers like huge, tall plants – there will finally be 18 of them. And the pillars inside the church were like a forest of strange trees. It *was* a complicated design, but I knew that I was making a very special building. And I wanted people to visit it from every part of the world.

◆ ◆ ◆

For me, the end came one evening in 1926. I was walking to a church to say my prayers. I was crossing the Gran Via, a wide road in Barcelona. I was thinking of my work and I didn't see a tram coming towards me. The driver of the tram wasn't able to stop in time.

For me, there was no time to say goodbye. But there was no need to say anything. Everyone in the <u>workshops</u> was busy. My team of builders, <u>sculptors</u> and painters all knew my wishes. The metal-workers knew what to do. The younger architects who helped me understood my design. For year after year, my work has continued. And one day, my basilica will be finished.

The Life of Antoni Gaudí

1852   Antoni Placid Guillem Gaudí i Cornet
       was born in Reus, a small town south of
       Barcelona, in Spain. He was the youngest
       of five children. Three of them grew up to
       be adults.

1863   At the age of 11, Antoni began studying at
       the Escuelas Pias of Reus.

1868   He moved to Barcelona and studied
       teaching in the Convent del Carme.

1873   He started studying at the Provincial School
       of Architecture in Barcelona.

1876   Antoni's mother and his brother, Francesc,
       a young doctor, died.

1878   Antoni finished his architectural studies.
       While he was studying, he worked
       for several architects and builders. He
       completed his three years of military
       service in Barcelona. Antoni designed
       some furniture which was shown at the
       Paris World Fair. The Catalan businessman
       Eusebi Güell liked his designs. It was the
       beginning of a friendship which won Gaudí
       many future commissions.

1879   He became a member of the *Centre Excursionista de Catalunya*. This was a group of people who visited places in Catalonia and France together.

1882   Antoni received a number of commissions from his patron, Eusebi Güell. These included: the *Bodegas Güell*; the *Palau Güell*; the *Pabellones Güell de Pedralbes*; the *Parc Güell*; and part of the Church of *Colònia Güell* in Santa Coloma de Cervello.

1883   He was commissioned to build a large Roman Catholic Church, the *Sagrada Familia*. He worked in his own personal 'organic' style. Work also began on an important house, the *Casa Vicens*, in Barcelona.

1888   He designed a building for the Transatlantic Company at the World Fair.

1889   Antoni designed the Bishops' Palace in Astorga.

1891–1892   He was given a commission to design the *Casa de los Botines* in Léon.

1895   Antoni designed the Güell Cellars in Garraf, Barcelona.

1898   He designed the *Casa Calvet* in Barcelona. The following year, the government of the City of Barcelona called this house the 'Building of the Year'.

1900   He designed the garden and houses of *Parc Güell*, and also a large house, *Casa Figueres*. Both of these projects were in Barcelona.

1902–1904   Antoni was commissioned to work on the repairs of the gothic Cathedral of Palma de Mallorca, La Seu.

1904–1910   Antoni built two of his most important works, the *Casa Batlló* and the *Casa Milà*. During that time, he also designed the Artigas Gardens.

1906   He started to live in his new home in *Parc Güell*, which was built by his assistant Francesc Berenguer. It is now the Gaudí Museum. In the same year, Antoni's father died.

1910   From this year, Antoni worked only on the Sagrada Familia. He spent the rest of his life on the project.

1918   His friend and patron Eusebi Güell died.

1925   Antoni began living in his workshop at the Sagrada Familia.

1926   Antoni was hit by a tram and died, aged 73, in Barcelona.

Pablo Picasso

• ◆ •

1881–1973

the most famous painter of the twentieth century

When you ask people to name a twentieth-century artist, my name is the first name they think of. My most important works are now sold for amazing prices.

◆ ◆ ◆

I was born in Málaga in Spain, on 25th October 1881. My father, who was a professor at an art school, helped me to draw and paint from a very young age. He helped me, and he often <u>criticized</u> me too. But soon I was very good at art. The teachers at the Barcelona School of Fine Arts thought that I was very good. At the age of 13, I became a student at that college.

It was interesting to learn about other artists, but I didn't want to copy them. I knew that I wanted to create my own style. When I was 16, I went to study at the Royal Academy of Fine Arts in Madrid, the capital city of Spain. I didn't stay there very long. I was bored because the teachers wanted me to do the same work as everyone else. I decided to leave the Academy. It was more useful to visit the *Museo del Prado* in Madrid. At the Prado, I studied the works of many important painters, especially works by El Greco.

Next, I decided to travel to Paris, the capital city of France. I met lots of interesting people there. Max Jacob – a poet, writer and painter – became my friend, and we decided to share an apartment. Life was hard for us – there wasn't much money and there wasn't much food. But I did create a personal style. For several years I painted many of my pictures with only blue and blue-green paints. In other ways, these paintings were simple pictures of their subjects.

♦ ◆ ♦

I returned to Madrid because I was very poor, and also because I'd become interested in politics. With Francisco Soler, I published *Arte Joven*, (Young Art), an art magazine which had a political message. I drew the pictures, mainly political cartoons. I signed my pictures with one name – Picasso. Well, my real name was a very long one – Pablo Diego José Francisco de Paula Juan Nepomuceno María de los Remedios Cipriano de la Santísima Trinidad Ruiz y Picasso. It needs two lines to write it! A short name was better on my cartoons. Also, I didn't want important people in Spain to know too much about me.

I wanted to change the <u>system</u> of government in my country, but it didn't happen. Perhaps the system changed *me*, in a strange way. At about this time, a rich American became my <u>patron</u>. She was the famous writer Gertrude Stein. She'd moved to Paris, where she created an art collection with her brother Leo. When I returned to France, I met the Steins. At their home, there were Saturday evening meetings of people who were interested in the arts. At these meetings I met several people who <u>commissioned</u> pictures from me.

At about this time also, I was painting with rose-red colours. My 'blue period' had finished and my 'rose period' had begun! And soon other influences appeared in my work–ideas from other cultures. The influence of African art was especially strong. A famous example of my 'African style' is my painting *Les Demoiselles d'Avignon (The Young Ladies of Avignon)*.

The Steins were helpful to me, but the most important help came from Daniel-Henry Kahnweiler. He opened an art gallery in Paris in 1907. He loved my work and sold many of my paintings from his gallery. A few years later, I made a famous <u>portrait</u> of him. Soon I was able to earn a good <u>income</u> from my work. I painted all the time. I painted people old people and young people, small people and large people, <u>acrobats</u>, dancers, and swimmers. I painted places – streets and restaurants, for example. And I painted many <u>still-life</u> pictures – flowers, guitars, hats, violins and wine bottles were all subjects for me. Work was mixed with pleasure because I often met my friends in cafés.

One person was especially important to me. She was Fernande Olivier, who I met in 1904. She became my model – I made many paintings of her. And she became my dear friend. During my life, I had many 'muses' like Fernande – young women who were both models and friends. Fernande was my most important muse until 1912. After that, Marcelle Humbert became my most important model.

By that time, I was painting in the style which was called 'Cubism'. Cubism was a style that my friend Georges Braque and I created. We tried new ways of showing three-<u>dimensional</u> objects in two-dimensional pictures. Cubism allowed us to show things in several ways at the same time. Marcelle Humbert appears in many of my first Cubist works. But unfortunately, she died when she was 30 years old.

◆ ◆ ◆

In 1914, the First World War began, and the German army <u>invaded</u> France. The war brought horror to the people of Europe, and no art could show their pain. In 1917, while the war continued, I went to Rome. I went there to design some <u>scenery</u> and <u>costumes</u> for a ballet called *Parade*. This ballet was performed by the dancers of Sergei Diaghilev's famous Russian Ballet Company. My designs used Cubist ideas, and some of my costumes were made of very thick paper.

While I was in Rome, I met Olga Khokhlova, a beautiful Ukrainian dancer in Diaghilev's dance company. We fell in love and on 12th July 1918 we were married. Our life together was never very peaceful. I painted and made designs and she danced. When Olga said that she was going to have a baby, I realized that my life was going to change. In February 1921, our son Paulo was born. Perhaps Olga and I weren't ready to be parents. Certainly, my artist's way of life was very different from Olga's way of life. So, my wife and I lived separate lives.

My next muse was Marie-Thérèse Walter. From 1927 to 1936, I painted her very often. And after that, Dora Maar came into my life. Dora was a photographer, but she also became my model. Olga and Dora hated each other, so life wasn't easy for me. But Dora inspired many of my paintings at that time, and also some of the poems which I wrote.

During 1935, my daughter Maya was born. Then in the later 1930s, war came again to Europe – a civil war in Spain. A group of men, led by General Franco, decided to replace the Republican government by force. Many people were killed and much of the country was destroyed in the fighting. In 1937, German aeroplanes bombed the Basque Country, the part of Spain near France. They did this because Hitler, the German leader, wanted to support Franco. Many people were killed. The Republican Government of Spain asked me to create a large picture to remind people of this horror. *Guernica* is the title that I gave it, because the village called Guernica was at the centre of the <u>destruction</u>. *Guernica* became my most famous painting.

◆ ◆ ◆

The Spanish Civil War, which Franco won, was the beginning of a much bigger problem for Europe. In 1939, the Second World War began. Once again, good people were fighting for <u>survival</u>. France was soon invaded, but I decided to stay there, in my second country. I didn't want to live in Franco's Spain. So I stayed in France, but I didn't <u>exhibit</u> any of my work. I met my next muse, Françoise Gilot, in 1944. And in that year, I also joined the French <u>Communist</u> Party.

When peace finally returned to the world, I was in my 60s. I began to work in many different styles. Sometimes I re-created styles from earlier centuries in my personal style. After the war, I decided to live in the south of France. I became a father twice more – to Claude in 1947 and Paloma two years later. Paloma later became a well-known fashion designer.

One day when I was 72 years old, I was working at the Madoura Pottery. I designed and painted <u>ceramic</u> works there. That day, I was visited by Jacqueline Roque, who was very interested in my work. At the time, she was only 27 years old but we became good friends. We became much closer after Olga died in 1955. Jacqueline became my second wife in 1961, when I was in my 80th year.

Jacqueline brought youth and beauty to my life in my old age. Our marriage lasted until my death on 26th June 1973. Jacqueline inspired more of my works than anyone else. During those last years, a wonderful thing happened. I was the first living artist to have an exhibition at the Louvre Museum in Paris. And there was time to think about my life in art. It was a rich life, both in art and in friendship.

The Life of Pablo Picasso

1881 Pablo Diego José Francisco de Paula Juan
      Nepomuceno María de los Remedios
      Cipriano de la Santísima Trinidad Ruiz y
      Picasso was born in Málaga, Spain.

1888 Pablo's father began teaching him drawing
      and painting.

1891 When he was ten, Pablo's family moved to
      Coruña Spain.

1895 After the death of Pablo's seven-year-old
      sister, Conchita, the family moved again,
      this time to Barcelona. Pablo's father
      worked as a professor of drawing at an art
      academy there. Pablo studied at the School
      of Fine Arts.

1897 Pablo, aged 16, became a student at the
      Royal Academy of San Fernando in
      Madrid, Spain.

1901–1904 Pablo chose to use his mother's surname,
      Picasso, for his work as an artist. He moved
      to Paris and shared an apartment with the
      journalist, Max Jacob. When he returned to
      Spain, he created the magazine, *Arte Joven*
      (Young Art) with his friend Francisco de
      Asis Soler. Later, Pablo had an exhibition in
      Paris. This period in his painting is known
      as the 'Blue Period'.

1904–1906	These years were Pablo's 'Rose Period'. He met the artist, Fernande Olivier, who became his model and his friend.
1906	He met the artist, Henri Matisse. They were friends until Matisse's death.
1907–1909	These were the years of Pablo's 'African style'. During this time, he painted one of his most famous works, *Les Demoiselles d'Avignon* (*The Young Ladies of Avignon*).
1909–1919	Pablo's 'Cubist Period'. In 1911, he met Eva Gouel, also called Marcelle Humbert, who became his muse until her death four years later.
1918	Pablo married the Russian ballet dancer, Olga Khokhlova. They had a son, Paulo, three years later.
1927	Pablo met Marie-Thérèse Walter. She became his next important muse.
1936	He met the French photographer and artist, Dora Maar. She became a model and a close friend.
1937	Pablo painted one of his most famous works, *Guernica*.

1939   During the Second World War, Pablo stayed in Paris when the Germans invaded the city. He continued to paint, but he didn't exhibit his pictures. He also wrote poetry, and during the next 20 years, he wrote more than 300 poems.

1943   Pablo met a young woman called Françoise Gilot, who was a close friend for several years.

1944   He joined the French Communist Party.

1950   Pablo was given the Stalin Prize for Peace by the Russian government.

1953   Pablo met Jacqueline Roque and they became close friends.

1961   He married Jacqueline and they stayed together until his death.

1962   He was given the Lenin Peace Prize.

1971   At the age of 90, Pablo became the first living artist to have an exhibition at the Louvre Museum in Paris.

1973   Pablo died aged 91, in Mougins, France.

Frida
Kahlo

◆ ◆

1907–1954

the woman who was famous for painting herself

I'm famous today for my colourful paintings – especially my <u>self-portraits</u> – which are some of the most famous art from my country, Mexico. And I'm also famous because I was married to another important Mexican artist, Diego Rivera.

◆ ◆ ◆

I was born in Coyoacán, a small town near Mexico City, on 6th July 1907. I was born in our family's house, *La Casa Azul* (The Blue House). My mother was my father's second wife. They had four daughters together, and I was their third child. But I had two half-sisters as well as my own three sisters. This was because my father and his first wife, who'd died at a young age, had two daughters together. So I grew up with females all around me!

My mother was a <u>religious</u> woman, and she always took us to church with her on Sundays. Sundays were peaceful days then. But some of my first memories are *not* peaceful ones – they are memories of the sound of guns! If we were in the street, and we heard guns, my mother picked me up and quickly ran to our house. The year 1910 was when this started happening.

As I grew up, I learned that we were living through the Mexican <u>Revolution</u>. <u>Revolutionaries</u> wanted to change our country's political <u>system</u>. The angry political arguments and the fighting lasted for many years. In those years, the fighting in the streets often made it difficult for us to live normally. For example, it wasn't easy to get food. Going to the shops was often too dangerous for us.

When I was six years old, I became seriously ill, which added to our problems. First, I started to feel very tired. I had no energy to do anything. I had to stay at home and rest. But the illness soon became worse. Our doctor told my mother that I had <u>poliomyelitis</u>. 'There's no <u>cure</u> for the illness,' he said, 'and your daughter will need a lot of help.'

My right leg became withered – it became thinner than the other one. Soon, it was very weak. I couldn't move it easily. Other children noticed this and they laughed at me. But I decided not to let my illness <u>interrupt</u> my life. When I was able to go to school, I tried hard at everything. My weak leg didn't stop me playing sports and enjoying my life again. At my first school, the classes which I enjoyed most were the art and literature classes.

The Mexican Revolution continued, and in 1914, the First World War started in Europe. That war lasted for four years, and as a result, there was less trade between Mexico and European countries. As a result, there were fewer things in the shops. But life went on, and in 1922 my hard work at my first school won me a place at the *Escuela Nacional Preparatoria*.

The *Escuela Nacional* was one of the most important schools in Mexico City, and I was one of only 35 girls there. My main interest at that time was in medicine. I wanted to become a doctor. At the school I found a lot of friends. My closest friend there was a young man called Alejandro Gómez Arias. And at that time, I first met the famous muralist, Diego Rivera. He was creating a mural called *The Creation*, in a building which I visited.

After I completed my time at the school, I wanted to explore the world. But in 1925, Alejandro and I were hurt in a serious accident. We were travelling in a bus which was hit by a tram. I was hurt very badly. In fact, I was very close to death. I was unconscious when I was taken to a hospital.

'Your leg is broken in eleven places,' said the doctor, when I finally woke. I looked at the bandages that covered my body, and I knew that the news was worse than the doctor had said. I soon learned that many other bones were broken too. But the injuries to my abdomen were the worst problem. As a result of those, I was never able to have children.

In the next few weeks, I had the first of a large number of operations – I had 35, in all. And for three months, my body was covered in <u>plaster</u>. Very slowly, I learned to walk, but the pain was with me for the rest of my life. As a result, I decided not to become a doctor. I decided to become a painter instead. I couldn't leave the house very often, but I could paint at home.

My mother had a special <u>easel</u> made for me, so that I could paint while I was lying in bed. My father gave me paints and brushes and I began to paint. The first picture which pleased me was a self-portrait - a painting of myself. I gave it to Alejandro. And that is how I began my journey as an artist.

◆ ◆ ◆

I completed 143 paintings during my career, and 55 of them were self-portraits. People often asked me why this was. 'It's because I'm so often alone,' I replied. 'I'm the subject which I know best.' And it's true that my life *was* lonely for a long time. But I had lots of time for thinking as well as for painting. At that time, though, I never painted my dreams. I didn't paint from my imagination, I only painted the <u>reality</u> of my life.

At last, however, I was strong enough to go outdoors. The revolutionaries had won the war in Mexico, and people began to hope for a better life. And people began to take an interest in my paintings. Soon, I met Diego Rivera again. I showed him some of my pictures and asked for his thoughts about them. I was surprised and pleased when he said, 'You have skill'. Diego gave me good advice, and after one of our meetings, he invited me to his <u>studio</u>. That was the start of a special relationship.

In 1929, Diego and I decided to marry. My mother didn't agree with our decision. Why? Diego was 20 years older than me and he wasn't a religious person. He didn't believe in any gods. My mother thought that there were too many differences between us. However, we shared many interests, and we were in love. I was sure that we were going to be happy together. We each had many other friends, and we spent time with them too. But we felt strong as a couple. Over the next few years we often spent time together in the great American cities where Diego painted murals in important buildings.

Diego and I believed in <u>communism</u>. We became friendly with the <u>communist</u> thinker Leon Trotsky, after he left Russia. Trotsky had been an important politician in Moscow, but he hadn't agreed with Stalin, the Russian leader. After that, his life was always in danger. During his visit to us in Mexico, Trotsky and I became very close friends. But one terrible day, he was killed by a man who Stalin sent to Mexico.

◆ ◆ ◆

When I found a completely personal style as an artist, my paintings used ideas from old Mexican culture and religious art, and also from Native American culture. I started to use brighter colours. I worked in a style that has been called <u>primitive</u>, but my work also used the ideas of <u>surrealism</u>. Many people liked my work and, as a result, I had a successful exhibition in the USA during 1938. A visit to Paris in the following year, led to another exhibition. And the best news of all was that the famous Louvre Museum bought one of my paintings.

It was an exciting time, because Mexican art was becoming known across the world. But during that year, 1939, another world war began. And as I returned home, sailing across the Atlantic Ocean, I had another reason for worry. After ten years, my marriage to Diego was failing. Perhaps we spent too much time apart. Perhaps we had too many other friends. Our marriage ended that year, but we still loved one another, and the next year – 1940 – we decided to get married again. We continued to argue and to make each other unhappy, but that was part of our life together. It seemed that we needed the arguments! We needed to make each other unhappy!

None of these problems stopped me from painting. I was busy during the 1940s. I painted a lot of pictures. And in 1943, I started teaching for the Mexican Education Ministry's School of Painting and Sculpture. Because my health wasn't very strong, I was able to teach my classes at home. People called my students 'Los Fridos'.

In 1952, I made some changes to my style of painting. I started work on a group of still-life pictures. But the pain from my old injuries was getting worse. My doctors gave me <u>drugs</u> to help me with my pain. Unfortunately, these drugs had a bad effect on my body. As my health got worse, part of my right leg had to be cut off. I learned to walk with an <u>artificial</u> leg, but this took a long time. Once again, I had to be alone a lot, and my painting helped me to feel better about this.

Painting helped me, but each day I had to fight for <u>survival</u>. Each little illness lasted longer. When I had a one-woman exhibition in Mexico City, I couldn't stand up. My bed was brought to the gallery where my pictures were hanging. I sat in bed while people looked at my work all around me.

I knew that death was coming closer. I wanted to use my time to do my best work. I hope that I succeeded. When I died, at my family home in Coyoacán, on 13th July 1954, I was only 47 years old. But in the years since my death, my work has become famous across the world.

The Life of Frida Kahlo

1907   Magdalena Carmen Frieda Kahlo y Calderón
       was born in her parents' home, called the
       Blue House, in Coyoacán, near Mexico City.

1913   At the age of six, Frieda became ill with
       poliomyelitis. Her right leg became withered.
       She attended the Colegio Alemán elementary
       school, in Mexico City.

1922   Frieda studied medicine at the *Escuela Nacional
       Preparatoria* (the National Preparatory School).
       She met Diego Rivera. Frieda became a
       member of the political group 'Los Cachuchas'.

1923   She began a close friendship with the leader of
       Los Cachuchas, Alejandro Gómez Arias. She
       changed the spelling of her name from the
       German 'Frieda' to the Spanish 'Frida'.

1925   Frida and Alejandro were injured in a serious
       accident, while they were travelling in a bus.

1926   Frida began to paint.

1927   She made many self-portraits, as well as
       portraits of family and friends.

1928   Frida met Diego Rivera again. Frida became
       a member of the Mexican Communist Party.

1929   Frida married Diego Rivera. Frida found
       her personal style when she painted her self-
       portrait called *Time Flies*.

1930–1931   The couple travelled to California where Diego painted murals in several cities. Frida painted *Frida and Diego Rivera*.

1932   Frida and Diego lived for a time in Detroit, where Diego was painting murals. Frida returned to Mexico to be with her ill mother, who died soon after.

1933   Frida travelled to New York, where Diego was painting a mural in the Rockefeller Center. Later, the couple returned to Mexico.

1935   Frida left Diego and lived alone in Mexico City.

1937   Four of Frida's paintings were shown in a public exhibition in Mexico City.

1938   Frida had a successful one-woman exhibition at the Julien Levy Gallery, in New York.

1939   Frida showed her work in Paris. Her self-portrait, *The Frame*, was purchased by the Louvre museum. She lived in Paris and became friends with the artists Pablo Picasso and Marcel Duchamp. Her marriage to Diego ended when Frida returned to Mexico. She moved back into her family home, the Blue House at Coyoacán.

1940   Diego left Mexico and went to San Francisco. Frida followed him, and they remarried there.

1943   Frida's health problems increased, but she began to teach for the Mexican Education Ministry.

1946   She was given the National Prize of Arts and Sciences for her painting, *Moses*.

1947   Frida's *Self-Portrait as a Tehuana* (*Diego in My Thoughts*) was shown at the National Institute of Fine Arts, in Mexico City.

1949   She wrote *Portrait of Diego*, which was published when an exhibition of her husband's work was shown at the Palace of Fine Arts, in Mexico City.

1952   Frida began painting a series of still-life paintings.

1953   She had her first one-woman exhibition in Mexico. Her right leg was cut off below the knee.

1954   Frida died, aged 47, at the Blue House, in Coyoacán, Mexico.

abdomen NOUN
the part of your body below
your chest

acrobat NOUN
someone who entertains people
by performing difficult physical
acts such as jumping and
balancing, especially in a circus

appoint VERB
to choose someone for a job or
a position

apprentice NOUN
a young person who works for
someone in order to learn
their skill

arrest VERB
to take someone to a police
station, because they may have
broken the law

artificial ADJECTIVE
made by people, instead of nature

bandage NOUN
a long strip of cloth that is
wrapped around an injured part
of your body to protect or
support it

belief NOUN
a powerful feeling that something
is real or true

bishop NOUN
a leader in the Christian church
whose job is to look after all the
churches in a particular area

brick NOUN
a rectangular block used for
building walls

cathedral NOUN
a large and important church

ceramic ADJECTIVE
made from clay (= a type of
earth) that has been heated to a
very high temperature so that it
becomes hard

ceramics PLURAL NOUN
objects made from clay (= a type
of earth) that has been heated to
a very high temperature so that
it becomes hard

chapel NOUN
a room or part of a church that
people pray in

civil war NOUN
a war between different groups of people who live in the same country

classical ADJECTIVE
of a style from ancient Greece or Rome, with columns and large arches

client NOUN
a person who pays someone for a service

commission NOUN
a request from someone to do a piece of work for them and be paid for it
VERB
to arrange for someone to do a piece of work for you

communism UNCOUNTABLE NOUN
the political idea that people should not own private property and workers should control how things are produced

communist NOUN
someone who supports the ideas of communism

costume NOUN
a set of clothes that someone wears in a performance

creative ADJECTIVE
using something in a new way

criticize VERB
to express your disapproval of someone or something

cure NOUN
a treatment for getting rid of a particular disease

destruction UNCOUNTABLE NOUN
damage that is so severe something cannot be used again or does not exist any longer

detail NOUN
one of the small, individual parts of something

detailed ADJECTIVE
containing a lot of details

dimensional ADJECTIVE
A three-dimensional object is solid. A two-dimensional object is flat.

dome NOUN
a round roof

dream (dreams, dreaming, dreamed or dreamt) VERB
to see events in your mind while you are asleep

dreamer NOUN
someone who looks forward to pleasant events that may never happen instead of thinking about what they are doing now

drug NOUN
a substance used as a medicine

easel NOUN
a stand that supports a picture
while an artist is working on it

exhibit VERB
to put an object in a public place
such as a museum so that people
can come to look at it

geology UNCOUNTABLE NOUN
the study of the Earth's structure,
surface and origins

geometry UNCOUNTABLE NOUN
a type of mathematics relating to
lines, angles, curves and shapes

gothic ADJECTIVE
of a style from the Middle Ages,
with high curved ceilings and
pointed arches

harp NOUN
A musical instrument that has
strings stretched from the top to
the bottom of a frame. You play
the harp with your fingers.

income NOUN
the money that a person earns or
receives

injury NOUN
damage to someone's body,
especially as a result of an
accident

inspire VERB
to give you new ideas and a
strong feeling of enthusiasm

instrument NOUN
an object that you use for making
music

interrupt VERB
to say or do something that
causes someone to stop what
they are doing

interruption NOUN
an occasion when someone is
interrupted

invade VERB
to attack and enter a country

inventor NOUN
someone who thinks of and
makes things that have never
existed before

local ADJECTIVE
in or from the place where you
live

make peace with VERB
to end an argument with
someone, especially by saying
sorry

mathematician NOUN
someone who is trained in the
study of numbers and
calculations

measuring instrument NOUN
a tool used for measuring
something

medieval ADJECTIVE
relating to the period of
European history between
A.D. 476 and about A.D. 1500

memorial NOUN
a structure that reminds people
of a person who has died

metalwork NOUN
the metal parts of something

military ADJECTIVE
relating to the armed forces of
a country

monastery NOUN
a building where monks live

monk NOUN
a member of a group of religious
men who live together in a special
building called a monastery

mural NOUN
a picture which is painted on
a wall

muralist NOUN
an artist who paints pictures
on walls

parachute NOUN
a large piece of thin material that
a person attaches to their body
when they jump from an aircraft
to help them float safely to the
ground

parliament NOUN
the group of people who make or
change the laws of some
countries

parliamentarian NOUN
someone who supported
Parliament in the English Civil War

patron NOUN
someone who supports and gives
money to artists, writers or
musicians

pipe NOUN
a long tube that a liquid or gas
can flow through

plaster NOUN
a hard white material worn on
an arm or leg to protect a
broken bone

poliomyelitis NOUN
a serious infectious disease which
can cause paralysis (= inability to
move parts of the body)

pope NOUN
the leader of the Roman Catholic
Church

portrait NOUN
a painting, drawing or
photograph of a particular person

primitive ADJECTIVE
very simple in style

proportion NOUN
the correct relationship between
the size of objects in a piece of
art

reality UNCOUNTABLE NOUN
used for talking about real things
rather than imagined or invented
ideas

religious ADJECTIVE
connected with religion

revolution NOUN
an attempt by a group of people
to change their country's
government by using force

revolutionary NOUN
someone who tries to cause a
revolution or who takes part
in one

rheumatic ADJECTIVE
causing swollen and painful joints

rights NOUN
things that you are morally or
legally allowed to do

scenery UNCOUNTABLE NOUN
the objects or the backgrounds in
a theatre that show where the
action in the play is happening

sculptor NOUN
an artist who makes solid works
of art out of stone, metal or
wood

self-portrait NOUN
a painting of yourself

still-life NOUN
a drawing or painting of an
arrangement of objects such as
flowers or fruit

studio NOUN
a room where someone paints,
draws or takes photographs

surrealism NOUN
a style in art and literature in
which ideas, images and objects
are combined in a strange way,
like a dream

surveyor NOUN
someone whose job is to examine
and measure land, especially
before buildings are built on it

survival UNCOUNTABLE NOUN
when someone or something
still exists after a difficult or
dangerous time

system NOUN
a way of working, organizing or
doing something that follows
a plan

trade NOUN
the activity of buying and selling
goods and services

unconscious ADJECTIVE
not awake and not aware of what
is happening around you because
of illness or a serious injury

version NOUN
a particular form of something

weapon NOUN
an object such as a gun, that is
used for killing or hurting people

wire NOUN
a long, thin piece of metal that
carries electricity

woodwork UNCOUNTABLE NOUN
the wooden parts of something

workshop NOUN
a place where people make or
repair things

Collins
English Readers

ALSO AVAILABLE IN THE AMAZING PEOPLE READERS SERIES:

Level 1

Amazing Leaders
978-0-00-754492-9
William the Conqueror, Saladin, Genghis Khan, Catherine the Great, Abraham Lincoln, Queen Victoria

Amazing Inventors
978-0-00-754494-3
Johannes Gutenberg, Louis Braille, Alexander Graham Bell, Thomas Edison, Guglielmo Marconi, John Logie Baird

Amazing Entrepreneurs and Business People *(May 2014)*
978-0-00-754501-8
Mayer Rothschild, Cornelius Vanderbilt, Will Kellogg, Elizabeth Arden, Walt Disney, Soichiro Honda

Amazing Women *(May 2014)*
978-0-00-754493-6
Harriet Tubman, Emmeline Pankhurst, Maria Montessori, Hellen Keller, Nancy Wake, Eva Peron

Amazing Performers *(June 2014)*
978-0-00-754508-7
Glenn Miller, Perez Prado, Ella Fitzgerald, Luciano Pavarotti, John Lennon

Level 2

Amazing Aviators
978-0-00-754495-0
Joseph-Michel Montgolfier, Louis Blériot, Charles Lindbergh, Amelia Earhart, Amy Johnson

Amazing Composers *(May 2014)*
978-0-00-754502-5
JS Bach, Wolfgang Mozart, Giuseppe Verdi, Johann Strauss, Pyotr Tchaikovsky, Irving Berlin

Amazing Mathematicians *(May 2014)*
978-0-00-754503-2
Galileo Galilei, René Descartes, Isaac Newton, Carl Gauss, Charles Babbage, Ada Lovelace

Amazing Medical People *(June 2014)*
978-0-00-754509-4
Edward Jenner, Florence Nightingale, Elizabeth Garrett, Carl Jung, Jonas Salk, Christiaan Barnard

Level 3

Amazing Explorers
978-0-00-754497-4
Marco Polo, Ibn Battuta, Christopher Columbus, James Cook, David Livingstone, Yuri Gagarin

Amazing Writers
978-0-00-754498-1
Geoffrey Chaucer, William Shakespeare, Charles Dickens, Victor Hugo, Leo Tolstoy, Rudyard Kipling

Amazing Philanthropists
(May 2014)
978-0-00-754504-9
Alfred Nobel, Andrew Carnegie, John Rockefeller, Thomas Barnardo, Henry Wellcome, Madam CJ Walker

Amazing Performers *(May 2014)*
978-0-00-754505-6
Pablo Casals, Louis Armstrong, Édith Piaf, Frank Sinatra, Maria Callas, Elvis Presley

Amazing Scientists *(June 2014)*
978-0-00-754510-0
Antoine Lavoisier, Humphry Davy, Gregor Mendel, Louis Pasteur, Charles Darwin, Francis Crick

Level 4

Amazing Thinkers and Humanitarians
978-0-00-754499-8
Confucius, Socrates, Aristotle, William Wilberforce, Karl Marx, Mahatma Gandhi

Amazing Scientists
978-0-00-754500-1
Alessandro Volta, Michael Faraday, Marie Curie, Albert Einstein, Alexander Fleming, Linus Pauling

Amazing Writers *(May 2014)*
978-0-00-754506-3
Voltaire, Charlotte Brontë, Mark Twain, Jacques Prevert, Ayn Rand, Aleksandr Solzhenitsyn

Amazing Leaders *(May 2014)*
978-0-00-754507-0
Julius Caesar, Queen Elizabeth I, George Washington, King Louis XVI, Winston Churchill, Che Guevara

Amazing Entrepreneurs and Business People *(June 2014)*
978-0-00-754511-7
Henry Heinz, William Lever, Michael Marks, Henry Ford, Coco Chanel, Ray Kroc

Collins
English Readers

Also available at this level

Level 2
CEF A2–B1

Amazing Aviators
978-0-00-754495-0

Amazing Composers
978-0-00-754502-5

Amazing Mathematicians
978-0-00-754503-2

Amazing Medical People
978-0-00-754509-4

Sign up for our emails at **www.collinselt.com**
to receive free teaching and/or learning resources, as well as the most
up-to-date news about new publications, events, and competitions.

⋐ POWERED BY COBUILD

www.collinselt.com   @CollinsELT   /collinselt

SUDDENLY SINGLE WOMEN'S GUIDE TO FINANCES

SUDDENLY SINGLE WOMEN'S GUIDE TO FINANCES

From Struggling to Secure Single, at Any Age

MIRA REVERENTE AND TRACY MARCYNZSYN

Copyright © 2015 Mira Reverente & Tracy Marcynzsyn
All rights reserved.

ISBN: 099664010X
ISBN 13: 9780996640107
Library of Congress Control Number: 2015913137
Reverie Press, Newbury Park, CA

DEDICATION

To all the single women out there, this is for you. Women and money are charged topics that everybody has an opinion about. Whatever your story, you have the power to take charge of your money. Save, spend, invest and share it with those you love. May the lessons of the women shared in this book help you to gain perspective, insight and valuable information about making money work for you.

A Special Thank You

You KNOW IT is a great idea when two single moms and former coworkers met at the dog park and realized they could write a book about their collective experiences and lessons learned through financial challenges of single womanhood and raising kids on mostly one income. And when we resolved to actually write the book, we decided self-publishing would be the best route to get this book into the hands of women who need it as soon as possible. Our only question was, "How will we pay for it?"

That's when we turned to our friends and family, our essential network of supporters, whom we count on in so many ways beyond financial, and asked them to believe in us by helping us fund our book. And so many of you said "yes." It brings tears of gratitude to our eyes when we think of the immense love and generosity that poured in from our loved ones, acquaintances and coworkers alike, pledging their support for our book through our Kickstarter campaign and making our vision a reality.

It's awe-inspiring to witness how a community can rise up around a project, with each person's contribution bringing it that much closer to achievement. It's empowering to see how, collectively, we can come together and help each other tackle challenges and accomplish our goals.

We thank you with all of our hearts for all of your love, support and generosity. It's because of your decision to take action and make a pledge to support us in our project that you're holding this book today. May it offer you or someone you care about useful information and inspiration to surmount any obstacles, knowing that we're all in this together and that we can do anything...with a little help from our friends!

Thank you!

Yash Abbas
Almond Aguila
Nancy Aguilar
Jose Alamillo
Liane and Erwin Alampay
Albert Alavera
Jamie Albanese
Jose Luis Alberto
Mian Alentajan
Joy and Don Alinea
Rob Altamirano

Arnold Alvarez

Manzar Amini

Joy and Florio Arguillas

Deborah Aron

Cecile and Jaime Ascalon

Cora Auste

Jay Austria

Benedict Balderrama

Mike Barber

Ligaya Barcenas

Vicki Brill

Anna Brillante

Sheldon Brown

Tisha Caeg

Jane and Ernivic Caparroso

Luisa and Aboy Castro

Susie Cervantes

Cor Cervera

Mimi Champion

Cathy Chien

Christina Childers

Bev Christian

Choy Corpin

Robert Cosico

Denise David

Henry De Guzman

Lily Delena

Carolyn De Leon
Jennifer De Leon
Angelo Ramon Del Fonso
Mimi and Albert Del Fonso
Joanne De Los Reyes
Doreen DeRoy
Jenine Diaz
Steve Doll
Doreen Downs
Sheli Ellsworth
Phil Enriquez
Ranz Erno
Marla Escobar
Monette Espinosa
Bambi Fabian
Beth and Steve Felsen
Charmagne and Rommel Feria
Glenn Fout
Salma Ghafari
Helen Glidden
Tawni Gomes
Jolie Gonzalez
Edith Gordoncillo
Kenneth Gross
Wendy Grossmann
Milly Gulamani
Becky Hall

Deanna Hallum
Rick Hawn
Kim Henderson
Shannon Henize
Katrina Hennessy
Noli Hernandez
Brenda Herron
Kate Heys
Deidre Hobbs
Ria Hofvenschiold
Masayo Honjo
Debbie Howarth
Apple Hurtado
Marie Israelite
Elizabeth Jaena
Joyce Javillonar
Doreen Jose
Ebong Joson
Laurie Kahn
Rick Kanatzar
Heather Karr
Shirley Kauffman
Youjin Kim
Amy Kuchherzki
Valerie Kulesa
Daria Lamborne
Bev and Bob Larson

Teri and Rodney Lee
Michelle Libman
Chilly Lopez
Tina Lott
Tintin Magbitang
Jaine Maglanque
Angela Magpantay
Mike Manalo
Regina and Eugene Mangawang
Rosalie and Dennis Mangoba
Mylene Manlogon
Dan Manuel
Maritess Mariano
Erly Maximo
Tom McKiernan
Mary McLemore
Patricia McNutt
Laarni Moreno
Francine Mossman
June and John Muller
Pochola Narvaez
Eileen and Reggie Necio
Christine and Caloy Nobleza
Monica Nolan
Ellen Nunez
Cindy O'Brien
Lisa Oliver

Susie Olsen
Sherry and Clark Osborne
Glenn Padilla
Carmela Pagay
Ramil Pangilinan
Violy Pantangco
Mike Parente
Emiko Parise
Chris Park
Anna Pascual
Anna Joy and Tino Pascual
Nancy Perez
Masmin Phelan
Lloyd Pilapil
Angeline Piotrowski
Leonard Pizarro
Aileen Platz
Christine Pollock
Michael Prades
Jennifer Quimson
Alan Rahmani
Larry Ramirez
Joel Ramos
Leah Raquino
Rodel Ravela
Leigh Reyes
Lorie Reyes

Orie Roman

Vicky and Ching Salazar

Deng San Valentin

Anna Santa Ana

Tom Schmidhauser

Anna Lia Severino

Edgardo Simondac

Orit Sinai

Ana Siscar

Sienna So

Susie and Lyndon Soriano

Josh Spiker

Becky Spring

Marilyn Stefano

Christine Steigelman

Denise Stevens

Tracy Lee Stum

Barbara Sullivan

Tetet Supan

Mavis Swann

Jen Swift

Janette Tabora

Linda and Tony Tan

Norbert Tan

Karlo Tatad

Letty and Rudy Timbol

Vanessa and Nicky Timbol

Jay Paul Tinio
Sarah Tolentino
Tasha Turner
April Ty
Jeanne Urquiza
Jing van Opstal
Peng and Vic Ventura
Anna Liza Vergara
Peachy and Paul Villacarlos
Rene Villafuerte
Robyn Wheeler
Fiona Yang
Paul Yapjoco
Iva Ybanez
Laura Ziff

CONTENTS

INTRODUCTION

"THE BEST ADVICE I ever got was from my hairdresser. She said, 'When it's over, it's over,'" recalled Stacey, a 50-year-old entrepreneur from Camarillo, California. Being faced with this truth is something so many of us have been through, and yes, it's hard to accept defeat and make the resulting changes that we need to move forward in our lives.

After 20-plus years of marriage, Stacey didn't want to admit it was over, despite the elephant in the room. Even after her divorce, she remained in denial about the end, until one day, it finally clicked, and she knew it was time to let go and get going with her life.

It's a familiar story, denying that the inevitable end is near (or here). But as all of the Staceys out there have found, when a relationship ends, it's time to move forward, as hard as it may be to leave the familiar life you (once) enjoyed with your partner. It makes it easier for us to accept such bitter truths when we trust that there is a reason for everything and that if it ended, it wasn't meant to be. Still, it's not easy to face these painful truths sometimes.

So now you're divorced, separated, widowed, newly single or seriously contemplating a change in relationship status. Now what?

A word of caution: This is no quick-fix book. We should know. We have both gone through break-ups, and some headaches and heartaches just refuse to go away, but we're slowly getting there. Did we say slowly? Yes, it's a very slow (and sometimes excruciatingly painful and tearful) process.

She remained in denial about the end, until one day, it finally clicked, and she knew it was time to let go and get going with her life.

To make matters worse, amid all of this tearful emotional pain, the bills still need to be paid, and you still need to eat (yes, you do), have a place to sleep and have clothes to wear (at the very least). Reorganizing your personal life is going to require some changes in your financial affairs as well. We know, you probably don't want to deal with it, and we get it. But the sooner you figure out the financial piece of your situation, the easier it will be to spend time healing and rejuvenating from the blow of new singledom.

While some of you may be independently wealthy (count your blessings!) or have access to the best legal and financial teams out there, that is not the case for most of us. We are lucky to have friends and family who offered support and helped us figure out several of the intricacies and complications in the murky world of cutting financial and emotional ties with a former beloved.

And so our experiences formed the fodder for this book, allowing us to create a compilation of the best advice and anecdotes we've received, plus some careful research and input from the experts.

If you aren't single yet but are considering it, this book is for you, too, so that you feel empowered moving forward. And believe us, if you don't already know this: You are not alone!

With some 41 million people widowed, divorced or separated and another 59.9 million who never married, according to 2000 U.S. census numbers (which have undoubtedly risen since then), women increasingly find themselves on their own and responsible for managing their money more than ever before (http://www.census.gov/prod/2003pubs/c2kbr-30.pdf).

We don't have to tell you that the world is changing. Gone are the days (for most of us) when our every need was met by someone else and "money" was a neutral term. Prince Charming might have come and gone, leaving us to fend for ourselves in so many ways, not the least financially. Like it or not, change happens, often without our consent, so learning how to handle life's transitions and all that comes along with taking care of ourselves in the best possible way can make life easier and more fulfilling.

No matter how you've come to find yourself flying solo, smoothly navigating your path involves making smart decisions and taking the right steps to protect yourself and ensure your best interests are met.

So how do you know if you're making the right choices? We found there aren't too many practical guidebooks for suddenly single women out there that extend beyond the emotional, despite the thousands of new divorcees annually who need this advice. We learned the hard way what (not) to do, and this book was born out of our, and many other single women's experiences.

Although we're not high-level financial executives—we're regular people—single moms who've had to figure out how to fend for ourselves and our children to learn how to support ourselves, on our own, on one income, the lessons we have learned through experience about what not to do, as well as what we wished we had known, are invaluable.

It's our hope that sharing some of our "wisdom born of pain" will prevent others from making the same mistakes. We've been there—we're still here—singles, surviving in what sometimes seems to be a sea of financial struggle. Security is the goal, and knowledge is the vehicle to get us there. You've heard the saying, "Knowledge is power," and so it is with money. The more you know, the more power you have to live life on your terms. Getting educated about how to make the most of your money is empowering, whether or not we find financial topics interesting. So we share our hard-found education humbly and with the hope that it will help support the single women out there to move from struggling and surviving to secure and thriving.

If you find yourself suddenly single, don't despair. Pick up our book and see how other women have managed to get from here to there. You've got this; you're not alone!

1

FINANCE 201

A good financial plan is a road map that shows us exactly how the choices we make today will affect our future.

—ALEXA VON TOBEL

A budget is telling your money where to go, instead of wondering where it went.

—DAVE RAMSEY

M ANY SUDDENLY SINGLE women find themselves in charge of their finances for the first time. And unless you lived in one of the few states that require financial education in high school, you likely learned all you know about finances on your own. While this isn't the case for all of us, money is often managed by the men in our lives, and we'd rather not worry about it. If this is you, the first step is to get yourself a basic education about finances.

This doesn't have to be intimidating, and, in fact, it is quite empowering. Living in the information age makes finding resources to learn about anything as easy as typing a few words into your Internet search engine. You might start your search by entering "managing money" or "money tips for women." Then you'll peruse the hundreds of sites listed about that topic. Skim through them and click on the ones that are relevant, bookmarking the best ones to read at your leisure. Of course, you can also read books on the topic for free at your local library or buy the ones you like best at a bookstore (half.com is a great online site to buy new and used books at great discounts) so you can take notes in them and reference them whenever you want. Online blogs and television programs about money (Suze Orman, Moneyline) are other great sources of pertinent financial information.

As you immerse yourself in the world of finance via online research, books, magazines and television shows, you'll start to increase your knowledge about money. As your money acumen increases, you will want to become more involved with managing money, because you'll feel more confident about how to manage money and finances in general. You may start out learning how to set a budget and pay off debt, progress to discovering saving and investment strategies and participate in long-term, big-picture issues, like saving for retirement and estate planning. Become a money-information sponge and soak up as much information about finances as you can.

Financial Planners or Advisers

Enlisting expert advice and guidance is also a great idea, in addition to your self-educating quest. Many financial planners will walk you through the basics and provide a financial needs analysis (FNA), explaining things like cash flow, expenses, debt management and the importance of setting up an emergency fund.

If your first thought (like ours) is, "How can I afford that?" take a deep breath and hear this: Financial planners differ in the way they bill for their services. While some financial planners charge from $1,000 to $3,000 to conduct an FNA, others bill hourly or charge a percentage of your net worth. Still others offer clients a free financial analysis and guidance. One financial planner we talked to (and because of multilayered regulations and a prohibitively long corporate-approval process when they're quoted, we decided to keep these financial experts anonymous) works for a company that operates on the premise that "no family should be left behind" when it comes to financial planning and education. And many financial planners work primarily with divorced and/or single women.

Getting a clear picture of where you are financially and how to get where you want to be is a huge financial milestone for countless people.

With the mission to "help families going through shifts," some financial planners educate their clients about finances through free, no-obligation financial needs analyses. Covering everything from the basics like budgeting and debt reduction to life and accidental-death insurance, asset accumulation, retirement, stocks, taxes and estate planning, including wills and living trusts, financial advisers help people assess their financial affairs. People are often surprised and relieved after consulting with an expert about their finances. Getting a clear picture of where you are financially and how to get where you want to be is a huge financial milestone for countless people.

Keep in mind that financial planners also need to make a living and receive compensation for their services. Financial planners who offer you fiscal direction for free are paid via commissions from insurers, investment companies and the various funds they encourage you to place your money with. However, these companies would not remain in business (and they are thriving like never before) if they were not providing a needed service in an ethical, responsible manner (and in accordance with a multitude of rules and regulations imposed on the financial industry).

"We put our mission before the commission," said one planner, adding, "We do the right thing for the client." Asking for a referral from a friend or family member who knows a good financial planner is often the best way to start.

Once you find a planner you trust, he or she will help you analyze your finances, set goals and make a plan for financial security that makes sense now and for the long term. If you feel resistance to contacting someone to help you, you're not alone. We tend to put this important step of assessing and organizing our finances off, or we haphazardly handle our money as we go.

While you may be quite capable of managing your own money, thank you, imagine how much better you can plan and manage it with an expert's advice and guidance. Tracy had a memorable and vivid dream while we were writing this book. A woman sitting at a small table told her to "Let the experts do their jobs and help you." That's good advice from dream world and in reality. Most of us don't question the need to hire a mechanic to fix our cars and keep them maintained and running their best. So why is there so much resistance to consulting with a financial planner about one of the most important areas of your life?

If or when you consult with a financial planner, don't stop educating yourself and being involved and interested in money issues.

That being said, if or when you consult with a financial planner, don't stop educating yourself and being involved and interested in money issues. You can listen to any advice given to you, but the bottom line is you have to be responsible for your choices about how to handle your money, and the more (ongoing) education you can get, the better you will be at making the best decisions for you. Getting a handle on finances is especially important for single women. Who is going to take care of you when you get old? It might be yourself, so the sooner you start planning for it, the better off you'll be in your golden years. Long-term care retirement accounts should be started sooner rather than later.

"Everyone's situation is unique," says one planner. "The cookie cutter approach isn't going to work for all of us," so talking to a financial planner about your specific situation and finances will yield the best return on your money.

In addition to finding and working with a financial adviser (see our Resources for contacts), we recommend reading financial publications of all types, from the traditional favorites like the Wall Street Journal, Forbes, Barron's and The Economist to online blogs like wealthysinglemommy.com, mydollarplan.com and dailyworth.com (send us some of your favorites!).

BUDGETING

Taking control by gaining a solid understanding of your finances starts with a budget. A big "B" word—bothersome, boring, bummer—to many of us, budgeting is key to unlocking your bright financial future. Whether you prefer to use a simple spreadsheet or go old school and opt for a notebook, setting a budget so you know exactly what's coming in and going out forms the foundation of your financial house.

Taking control by gaining a solid understanding of your finances starts with a budget.

Smartphone applications like Mint, Goodbudget, Mvelopes, Expensify and BillGuard are just some of the popular free budgeting and money-management apps available on iOS and Android operating systems.

Found Money

Demystifying where your money goes—it's so easy to lose track of the bi- or tri-weekly trips to Starbucks or the monthly pedicures—will put you on the right track. Getting clear about your spending enables you to rein in and control unnecessary expenses. When you set a budget, you can clearly see whether you're not supposed to spend anything more on groceries for the month of June, for example. But maybe there's wiggle room in another category like dining out. Flexibility is fine as long as you keep the balance in check. Take or add from your estimated spending in each category as you need to adjust it; it is your money to make decisions about, after all, and you know your priorities.

Getting clear about your spending enables you to rein in and control unnecessary expenses.

I have a dear friend who told me that she can't afford the monthly membership fee at a neighborhood gym. While we were looking at areas where she might have some wiggle room, she realized she could cut the twice-a-month, $80-per-time housecleaning to just once a month, and she joined the gym with her found "extra" money! This is also a great example of how talking things over with a trusted adviser and/or friend can yield solutions faster than you think!

CHILD'S PLAY

Involving your children in the budgeting process is a great idea for many reasons. They can—and need—to understand why it's important to have a budget and the powerful role they play in relation to it. My daughter always looks forward to our girl time. She knows it's a special mommy-and-me time when no one else is invited. It's just the two of us. So I remind her about our date one or two days before and give her a choice: a movie and a home-cooked dinner or dinner out, but no movie. Every once in a while, we'll do both, say on her birthday or mine or if someone gave us a gift card to use. If she wants to do something else, like visit a museum, I'll say, "We'll go to the museum, but then we'll skip the movie this time. Maybe next month?"

> *Involving your children in the budgeting process is a great idea.*

In our family, we have a fun way of saving our spare change in what we call our Abundance Jar. We use the cool-shaped bottles from POM Wonderful pomegranate juice. Whenever we have extra change or find a coin, it goes into the Abundance Jar. It's fun to watch it fill up surprisingly quickly and then to take the change when it's full, pour it into the change machine, and turn it into bills before spending it on something abundantly fun and family-oriented, like getting ice cream or going to the movies. There's something valuably tangible and concrete about watching those little coins collected and turned into fun money! It illustrates how every little bit adds up and how, with a little savings and patience, we can live abundantly with our spare change. I know this is a childhood memory my kids will carry with them and probably carry on.

My teenage son recently started his own Abundance Jar—using a larger POM bottle than the one we share—for his own change and tips from work. It's so rewarding when our kids pick up those healthy little habits we teach and take it up a notch too. Involving kids and giving them an important role in saving money develops lasting lessons for life.

Label It

There are myriad ways to organize your budget, but every budget should include labels or tags for necessities and discretionary expenses. The mortgage or rent falls under necessities, as do utility bills. Discretionary expenses are items we can live without, like dining out and recreation. When you set a budget, figure out which expenses are necessary or discretionary and go from there. If you have a large total for discretionary expenses, maybe move a few hundred dollars or so to a savings account or pay off debt.

Our Resources section lists several great books and resources for finding detailed information about all things budgeting. We'd love to add some of your favorite new discoveries to our list, so share your finds with us on our Suddenly Single Facebook page: facebook.com/SuddenlySingleForWomen. When you unearth those perfect gems, you know others can benefit from them too.

Reducing Debt

Unfortunately, debt is very commonplace (just look at our national debt) and increasingly easier to get into these days, especially consumer debt, courtesy of credit cards mostly. But did you know that there's good and bad debt?

According to David Bach, author of the *Finish Rich* book series, when you purchase something that immediately goes down or depreciates in value, that could be classified as bad debt. Furthermore, bad debt has no potential to appreciate or increase in value.

Your mortgage and student loans both fall under good debt. Credit cards, store credit cards and car loans are categorized as bad debt. As a general rule, you can use good debt to get rid of or reduce bad debt. Say you take out a home equity loan at 5% interest to pay off credit card debt with an 18% interest rate. That's turning bad debt into good debt.

When you buy a flat-screen TV using a credit card, for example, and only make minimum or partial payments, you are accumulating bad debt. The flat-screen TV is depreciating and losing its value long before you ever pay it off.

As a general rule, you can use good debt to get rid of or reduce bad debt.

The key is to use credit or store-issued credit cards sparingly or only if you can pay them off at the end of the month or soon after. Learn how to differentiate between wants and needs. A flat-screen TV is a want, but food is a need. Also, save the use of credit cards for emergencies like car repairs if you haven't started or built up your emergency fund yet.

Don't feel bad or beat yourself up if you are in debt (I'm reassuring myself as I write this). As a single mom, I know too well how handy that Kohl's or J. C. Penney card is when my daughter needs black pants and new shoes at the last minute for a chorus performance or my son needs a dress shirt tomorrow and finds he's outgrown the few he owns. I know I will pay these off, and I use them when I need to. There will be a day, sooner than I want to believe, that my kids will be grown, and then I'm sure I'll be rich—or at least hit up for unexpected expenses less often!

Thankfully for us, money gurus have shared several strategies for reducing and eliminating debt, regardless of your budget constraints. Tactics include paying the cards with the highest interest rates with the most money you can while making only the minimum payments on the rest of the cards, as well as paying off the cards with the lowest balances first to establish momentum. As you pay off each card, you add the amount you were paying for its minimum payment to the amount you pay on the next card. Check out the listings in our Resources section to find the books we like best about paying off debt.

Saving Money

I'd venture to guess that more of us than we'd like to admit have little to show at the end of the day for our hard work. The money comes in, and the money goes out. That's true for people in every tax bracket. Even people who earn millions each year via their paychecks carry debt and overextend themselves.

How wonderful would it be to save some of that hard-earned dough? The Rule of 72 may inspire you, as it did us, to figure out a way to save money. The Rule of 72 demonstrates how long before money can double given a fixed annual rate of interest.

Here's how it works: Divide the interest rate on your money by 72 to determine how long it will take to double your money.

For example: If your money earns 10% interest, divide 72 by 10, and you'll see that it will take 7.2 years to double your money!

At 6% interest, divide 72 by 6, and your money will double in 12 years. This illustrates the power of compound interest.

Divide the interest rate on your money by 72 to determine how long it will take to double your money.

EMERGENCY FUND

Most finance professionals will recommend that you save anywhere from three to six months' worth of living expenses that you can access easily at any time you need to. Suze Orman says you should have eight months of living expenses saved. This is your emergency fund and your peace of mind. If your monthly expenses are $3,000 a month, you want to have anywhere from $9,000 to $18,000 ($24,000 by Suze's standards) in an easy-to-access account.

Most people, including single women like us, find it difficult to impossible to stash away that much extra money. But remember, you just have to start somewhere. It could be $100 this month and $200 next month when you get that extra project. Just keep socking money away anytime you see the chance. It's even better if you automate it and send $50 to your emergency fund automatically from your checking account.

You can also draw from this account when you get hit with an unexpected, huge plumbing bill. I did! Or when you have that emergency car repair. You will stress less—believe me. Get started and do it now. Every little bit gets you closer to your goal. And setting goals is the first step to achieving them.

Retirement

With life expectancy higher than ever before, saving enough money for retirement is a must. While in the past, people depended on Social Security, pensions and investments to finance their golden years, that formula won't keep you afloat in today's world. Statistics show that Social Security is an outdated system that cannot sustain itself, as the numbers of people paying into and collecting from the fund have changed drastically since the program began in 1937. Whereas some 45 workers used to pay into the system for every one person collecting (retirees), today, the number of workers paying into the Social Security system is drastically reduced to five workers per every retiree collecting.

You can leverage your money and make the most of it by working with an expert who is knowledgeable about the best investments, tax breaks and money habits.

Additionally, many businesses don't offer pensions like they used to, so the old model of working for one company for the better part of your career and then retiring on your pension is fast becoming a distant memory.

Tack on to that staggering consumer debt carried by so many of us and poor savings, and you've got a financial mess on your hands.

With the state of affairs such as they are, maximizing your money is a must. You can leverage your money and make the most of it by working with an expert who is knowledgeable about the best investments, tax breaks and money habits. Our Resources section offers some good books on the topic.

If you work for a company that offers a 401(k) and they will match a portion of your contributions, you should definitely take advantage of that. It's essentially free money. By withholding through payroll deduction, most people can save up to $18,000 of pretax income in 2015 ($24,000 if you are 50 years old or older). Even if you leave the company, you can roll the money over or open your own individual retirement account (IRA). For teachers and employees of nonprofit groups, the equivalent of a 401(k) is the 403(b).

You can also open an IRA whether or not you have a 401(k). However, you won't be able to deduct your IRA contributions from your taxable income if you earn more than $71,000 annually (single filers) or $118,000 (married filing jointly). If you don't have a retirement plan at work, you can get the full deduction no matter what your income is, unless you are filing jointly and your spouse has a retirement plan at work. You can contribute up to $5,500 annually to an IRA or $6,500 if you're over 50.

Then there's the Roth IRA, where you contribute after-tax dollars and get no tax deduction for your contributions. The main advantage of the Roth IRA over the traditional IRA is that your money grows tax-free, and there is no tax for withdrawals after the age of 59½. There is also no mandatory withdrawal at age 70, unlike the traditional IRA. You can withdraw your contribution at any time, penalty-free and tax-free, but not your earnings. The only caveat is that you must make less than $131,000 (single) or $193,000 (married filing jointly).

Dubbed "the next big retirement option" by several money and finance publications, an annuity is simply an insurance product that pays out income. An annuity can be part of an individual's overall retirement strategy, and it is a popular choice for those who would like a steady income during retirement. Income from an annuity can be received monthly, semiannually, annually or in a lump-sum payment. There are a few types of annuities: immediate versus deferred and variable versus fixed. While there is no annual contribution limit to an annuity and your contributions are tax deferred, there are fees, surrender charges and commissions associated with it. Read the fine print.

Don't get overwhelmed by the acronyms and big words. And check with your accountant or the IRS website for the exact tax breaks relating to your income level. Also, the already complex rules pertaining to retirement accounts tend to change over time. We are just giving you a basic overview.

WHAT IF IT'S TOO LATE?

I recently met an endearing, friendly woman at the dog park; I'll call her Shirley. "It's too late for me," she told me. "Your book is too late for me. I didn't start saving early enough." (She's probably in her early 60s). "I have no 401(k) or retirement. When I went to get my Social Security, I said, 'Excuse me? How is that going to support me?' They told me, 'You were supposed to save, Ma'am. Have a nice day.'"

Don't lose hope. There is a way to make it work by thinking creatively.

We can be sure that Shirley's not alone in this predicament. She does own a home in a nice, coveted area, though. As a single mother decades ago, she was able to work, raise her two kids solo AND BUY A HOME. So all's not lost, I told her. She told me she didn't think she could survive today on her own, but women are smart and strong, and we figure it out, especially when kids are involved. She did it back then, and she (we) can do it now.

So where's the best place to start if you find yourself retired without savings? This is where creativity, innovation and out-of-the-box thinking come into play. The first step is to get professional advice from a financial planner who won't charge you to point you in the right direction but will give you a clear picture of your finances.

Beyond that, creative solutions exist. Everybody's case is different. In Shirley's case, with a three-bedroom home in a nice neighborhood, she could feasibly rent out some rooms to start bringing in at least $1,000 extra a month, which she can start investing right away so that it starts growing. Look at your assets. Maybe there's furniture or other possessions you don't want, use or love anymore that you can turn into cash to invest and grow. Do you have a luxury car you can trade for something reliable and less costly?

Don't lose hope. There is a way to make it work by thinking creatively. For example, with the increasing numbers of senior citizens, creative housing options make sense. Seniors can pool their funds and buy houses where they can all live together, creating a built-in community of support and companions while securing an affordable home. Have you heard of the Tiny House movement? This is just the beginning of an evolution in housing to bring simple, affordable options to the forefront.

Don't take no for an answer and don't curl up in a ball and cry (at least not for too long).

Necessity has always been the mother of invention, and this situation is no exception. If you don't see what you need existing, create it! Don't take no for an answer and don't curl up in a ball and cry (at least not for too long). There is always a solution, no matter the problem. Remember to enlist a friend's help to brainstorm all your options, including the ones you'd never think of on your own.

Estate Planning

In most states, if you're single and you die without a will, your assets or estate will go to your nearest relatives. This can be disconcerting if you wanted or had every intention to pass them on to your significant other, longtime partner or friend.

Even if you're still alive and become incapacitated, without a spouse at the ready to represent you, a judge might appoint a relative to make medical and financial decisions for you. And there's an even worse scenario: If you have no living relatives, a stranger may be appointed by a judge to make those important decisions for you.

Create a will and a revocable living trust.

To avoid the above scenarios, ConsumerReports.org advises singles to do the following:

- Create a will and a revocable living trust. A revocable living trust will provide instructions on how and where you want your assets to be distributed when you die. Unlike a will, a living trust lets a successor trustee distribute your assets to beneficiaries you named without going through probate, which is a public court proceeding.
- Update beneficiary designations. It is good to update this every few years or so or after major life changes

such as a divorce or widowhood. The person named as a beneficiary on investment accounts and insurance policies will inherit those assets, even if he or she is not named in your living trust or will.

- Draw up powers of attorney. Without a signed authorization, unmarried partners or a friend cannot make medical and financial decisions, unlike married people. Make it a priority to choose a person you would like to act on your behalf. Choose someone trustworthy and capable. Do it now.

- Check the laws in your state or, better yet, consult with an estate-planning attorney to find out how to draw up powers of attorney. With an advance health care directive, you can designate someone to make health care decisions for you in the event that you become unable to do so. This legal document will also contain your wishes, such as life-sustaining treatment, organ donation and funeral arrangements. Once this document is drawn up, make several copies and give them to your family members, lawyer, doctor and designee or health care proxy, the person who will make medical decisions for you in case you are incapacitated.

If hiring a professional is out of the question, look online for plenty of options, such as LegalZoom.com.

LIFE INSURANCE

According to research conducted at the University of Virginia's Darden School of Business and Genworth Financial, almost 70% of single parents living at home have no life insurance.

The surveys indicate that single parents are not buying life insurance because of two primary reasons: It is too costly, and it is too complicated to shop around. Guilty as charged! Furthermore, the study indicates that most single parents are too busy or too scared to think about their life insurance needs. Single moms, especially, are more likely to be uninsured than single dads. Guilty again!

Buy coverage now. Research whether a term policy is good for your needs.

Before the unthinkable happens to you, consider these tips:

- **Investigate.** Check with the noncustodial parent if he/she is carrying life insurance. Where is it held, and are your children the beneficiaries? How much is his/her coverage?
- **Assess.** Figure out how much you need for yourself. A rough rule of thumb is 6 to 10% of your annual salary. Consider adding more to cover your mortgage, the kids' college education and funeral costs.

- **Buy coverage now.** Research whether a term policy is good for your needs. Comparison shop. Ask friends and family what they have. Don't wait for prices to drop. Quit smoking. Studies have also shown that prices are rising for smokers.
- **Share.** Information is useless unless you share it. Let your family members know where your policy is. Keep insurance documents safely stored with the rest of your estate documents.

LONG-TERM CARE

According to the American Association for Long-Term Care Insurance (AALTCI), in 2013, insurance rates for women rose 20 to 40% while rates for men dropped by 15%.

Blame longevity. Women are outliving men by five to seven years now, which means we need benefits longer. Since insurance prices are based on risk, women are paying more.

Women are outliving men by five to seven years now, which means we need benefits longer.

DISABILITY INSURANCE

Have you ever heard the saying, "Your income is your most important asset?" Having said that, you need to insure your income, and this is where disability insurance comes in.

If you have to choose, most experts would recommend choosing short term since most disabilities are usually short term.

Check with your employers to see if they offer this benefit. If not, consult a professional about how much disability insurance you need for your situation. Disability policies usually come in two forms: short term and long term. If you have to choose, most experts would recommend choosing short term since most disabilities are usually short term.

As with most insurance policies, the premium for disability insurance is usually fixed. The younger you are when you purchase a policy, the lower your premium will be. One thing worth considering is the "own occupation" rider, which simply means that disability insurance will pay if you are unable to perform your own occupation, even if you can do other jobs.

Disability insurance is just one more way to ensure your independence and take care of yourself, no matter what may happen in the future. It is especially crucial for single parents who don't have a spouse's income to help cover the gap.

The Good News

There's so much to deal with when you're single, but the good news is you don't have to do it all on your own. That's why experts exist. Let them do their jobs and help you.

You don't have to do it all on your own.

Financial advisers, as we learned while writing this book, are out there to help you get your finances in order and formulate a financial plan for free! Of course you're capable of figuring it out on your own, but why not maximize your money and options by talking to an expert? You probably don't think twice about calling a plumber to fix your burst pipe (though, no doubt, some of you can fix it yourselves), so why not take your finances to the people who specialize in them?

Check with your friends or families for a referral for a financial planner, or do an online search. Our Resources section and website also have referral information and contacts for financial planners.

2

Our Stories

A woman is like a tea bag—you never
know how strong she is until she gets in
hot water.

—Eleanor Roosevelt

Turn your wounds into wisdom.

—Oprah Winfrey

Mira's Story

I THOUGHT I HAD finally met my dashing prince when I married my college sweetheart, but we didn't live happily ever after.

We got divorced after two children, 16 years of marriage, and a move from halfway around the globe. While the reasons for our divorce don't matter now, suffice it to say that I wasn't prepared. Who prepares for divorce anyway? I should probably have left him earlier, but having grown up in a predominantly Catholic country, I thought that the stigma associated with divorce was unnerving and shameful, at the very least. It gnawed at my conscience for so long. I thought I had failed my parents, my in-laws, my friends, my upbringing, the nuns at the Catholic schools I attended and the priest who married us.

I had two young children, a few part-time jobs and a mountain of debt, courtesy of my ex. I was beyond overwhelmed, but I decided to trudge on. This is where years of hiking and marathon training kicked in. I had to constantly remind myself to put one foot in front of the other and take each day as it came. "Just one more mile," or "The summit is just around the corner" were mantras I often recited to myself as I tackled bills, paperwork, and the gamut of emotions often associated with the end of any relationship, much less my marriage.

Even before my divorce was finalized, I knew I wanted to remain in this SoCal suburb where I have built a life, nurtured friendships and made important connections in my career. I make ends meet by taking in a couple of roommates. I also cut down on nonessentials like premium cable, a landline, magazine subscriptions and so forth. My daughter and I live simply. I cook almost every day, clean my own house and walk my own dog.

We save up for the occasional movie and dinner out. I am a proud mommy when I can teach my daughter how to make sound financial choices: watch a movie or have dinner out; buy a book or borrow from the library; have a birthday party or save the money for a trip.

One big thing we look forward to every year is our summer road trip. We drove to Vancouver last summer and stayed with friends along the way, making two- to three-day stops in San Francisco, Portland and Seattle before reaching our destination in Vancouver. This year, we hit the national parks in Utah and Arizona for some hiking. To save money, we stayed in a charming (think small, no electricity, outhouses, etc.) bunkhouse we found on AirBnB.com located near the Arizona-Utah border.

I love my life more than ever now, even if an important, long-term relationship ended to make me flourish. As I have been told many, many times, there is always a lesson somewhere in there. You may not see it right away behind tear-filled eyes, but there are lessons to be gleaned from every setback, disappointment or heartache.

What were my lessons? That I shouldn't be too dependent on one person. I used to be overwhelmed by financial statements of all kinds. I left that part up to my ex to deal with. The statements from brokerage and investment firms baffled me like they were written in Arabic or another foreign language. I embrace them now. I compare several months' worth of statements and call my banks when I have a question. I have learned to analyze and compare interest rates and know exactly what my rates are and how much I still owe on my house and car.

I also learned that true strength comes from within, and there is a limit to grief. Friends will come and go. They will get tired of your constant venting and bashing of your ex, but you will prevail on your own. You just have to make peace with that and draw strength from within or from sources like your religion, meditation, or physical fitness.

I have also learned to let go. My 17-year-old son's decision to live with his dad might have broken my heart in a million little pieces, but I take comfort in the fact that children will leave the nest sooner or later. His was a bit sooner than I had anticipated, but I know he is in good hands and probably needs his dad more now that he is going through the challenges of young adulthood.

Lastly, I have learned to forgive and forget. If you know me well, you know that I don't forget easily, but I have forgiven. As someone told me recently, "Don't let bitterness hold you back."

TRACY'S STORY

I made the decision to leave my children's father and move from Kauai to California when my kids were one and four years old. It's been a learning experience, to say the least, but somehow I've managed to keep my kids in our upscale community throughout their school careers. My 17-year-old son recently graduated from high school and is now thoroughly enjoying his college experience, while my 14-year-old daughter is just starting high school. Both kids are loving, smart, polite, caring, capable and kind people whom I'm proud to call my children.

I've supported them on my own, with minimal help from family, for 13 years. It has not been easy housing and raising two children on one paycheck in this part of California, and I've learned all kinds of ways to make and stretch dollars during these lean years.

When I first moved back to California from Kauai, I moved in with my sister and brother-in-law while I looked for an affordable place to live, which may well be an oxymoron in this area. Fortunately, I had applied and been approved for a housing voucher through a federal program with the US Department of Housing and Urban Development (HUD). Known as Section 8, this housing voucher allowed me to locate a safe and comfortable place to live for me and my children, despite my not having a job (or money) at the time. Many people don't know that this program exists and, even more, that it is portable, meaning you can apply for it in one state and move with it to another state.

This program was a lifesaver for me, as it enabled me to leave an unhealthy relationship and relocate to a safe and stable home. Once our housing was settled, I was able to look for and find a job. My son entered kindergarten, and I enrolled him in after-school daycare so I could work; I found a wonderful, caring babysitter for my daughter through an organization that also helps fund childcare for single, working parents. I soon found a job teaching classes at our local community center and later secured full-time employment at an academic publishing company.

After almost a year working at the publishing company, I decided to become a freelancer rather than an in-office employee with my company, as I didn't like the long hours away from my children (even though they were in good hands, I wanted to be as involved with raising them as possible). I believe becoming a freelancer and working at home was the best parenting decision for me. I was able to work at home and then pick up my son after school. As my daughter got older (and became potty trained), I enrolled her in a wonderful preschool part time, which allowed me to focus on work and also to spend many daytime hours with her.

In addition to freelancing, I found other ways to generate income that didn't require me to spend hours on end in an office away from my kids. Some of these jobs included working as a community coordinator for an exchange student program, which paid on a commission basis, selling items on eBay and editing and writing various projects I found through Craigslist.

As my kids got older, and my daughter also entered school, I was able to work more hours guilt-free. Eventually, I secured a couple of (mostly) great telecommuting positions and was able to move out of our Section 8 apartment and into a house.

In order to make ends meet financially, I shared a four-bedroom house with another single mother, and we split expenses such as utilities and rent so that we could live in a great neighborhood in a wonderful house with a pool. Sharing a house is not without its trials, but we were able to peacefully coexist and work out any problems by communicating.

Today, in addition to a full-time, telecommuting editing job, I work as a freelance editor and writer. Not being tied to an office allows me flexibility and control of my schedule, and I can pick up my kids after school and be there with them to help with homework and just hang out with them.

I am still working on building up a savings account and reducing debt, but we have what we need, including a place to call home (renting), food to eat and clothing to wear. We also manage to splurge here and there on Starbucks, movies, sushi and little extras. My kids also appreciate these extra things more than some of their friends who seem to have it all, all the time, and they have an awareness about money and how much things cost.

Despite the struggles, I am living proof that no matter how bleak the picture, you can figure it out and make it work. We know that where there's a will, there's a way.

My best advice is to not be afraid to ask for help. Whether you need resources, a referral or financial assistance, ask, and ye shall find. There are countless organizations out there to help you; sometimes finding them is the biggest obstacle, but don't give up. We are not alone, even if it feels that way sometimes. Ask for help. Don't be ashamed; you don't need to suffer.

And remember that there is always a reason for your experiences, so be optimistic—and don't give up—maybe they'll help you write a book someday about what you've learned, for example!

3

GETTING YOUR HOUSE IN ORDER

Money is only a tool. It will take you
wherever you wish, but it will not
replace you as the driver.

—AYN RAND

Orderliness begets wealth.

—SUZE ORMAN

IT'S NATURAL TO get overwhelmed as our lives as we know them are unraveling. I'm sure we all know a friend or two who just signed on the dotted line because they thought they had no other option or just wanted it to be over.

Deena is one such example of a woman who just wanted out and, in her rush to get out of Dodge, sold herself too short in the divorce settlement. Married for 18 years and the mother of three kids, Deena finally had enough of her husband's alcohol-driven physical abuse.

"I wanted out at all costs. 'Where do I sign?'" Deena asked her husband's divorce lawyer, who agreed to represent them both "to save money." Deena thought she'd made out great, settling for a $50,000 cash settlement and $1,000 a month in child support. She assumed the car her husband bought her for her birthday would be hers without question and, having never lived on her own, thought the settlement money would support her for years to come.

Don't use your husband's divorce attorney, no matter how amicable the divorce is.

Was she in for a surprise when she learned "her" birthday gift car, registered and titled in her husband's name, was not part of her deal. And she soon found out that $50,000 is not that much money, especially when you're raising kids. Deena's ex-husband, on the other hand, was not experiencing any financial stress from the divorce. He had plenty of stocks, three homes, a pension, an IRA and a stockpile of savings, all assets the couple shared while they were married.

Had Deena been properly represented, she would have been advised not to sign away her rights to assets from which she was rightfully entitled to benefit—as her husband was. Instead, she is a struggling single mother, and while the kids are in college or living out of the house now, she is still living paycheck to paycheck with no financial security to show for all those years she helped her husband further his career and raised three kids as a stay-at-home, loving and involved mother and homemaker.

Let this be a lesson to you: Don't use your husband's divorce attorney, no matter how amicable the divorce is and how friendly he or she seems. Find your own representation. Ask family or friends for a referral or search online for a reputable divorce attorney in your area whom you feel comfortable talking with. One well-known online source to locate an attorney is martindale.com, which provides information about lawyers in your area. As eager as you may be to flee a bad situation, think before you leap. Be smart, know your rights and secure good representation through a knowledgeable attorney (see Questions for Your Attorney in the Appendix).

You can also find pro bono legal groups in your area and check whether you qualify for free or sliding-fee legal help. In our area, we have the Ventura County Bar Association (vcba. org), but there are some cases they cannot help with—foreclosure, child support, and bankruptcy, among others. No walk-ins are allowed, and there is a $35 administrative fee for a 30-minute consultation as of this writing. So read the instructions on the website and call first.

WHAT YOUR LAWYER OR MEDIATOR DIDN'T TELL YOU

"I wish my lawyer would have had a simple timeline of events. I kept getting packets and packets of papers in the mail, and they were getting overwhelming."

—STACEY S., CAMARILLO, CALIFORNIA

"Our mediator was great! She helped me understand that I owned 50% of everything—even if my ex-husband felt he owned everything."

—LENN M., NEW YORK, NEW YORK

In order to ensure fair and accurate representation, some states don't allow an attorney to represent both parties in a divorce. Your attorney should have your best interests in mind when negotiating your divorce settlement.

Things like income, assets, debts, children, child support, alimony and visitation schedules need to be addressed and split fairly. This is one reason to find an attorney who specializes in divorce; an experienced, ethical divorce attorney will be sure that all of these essential issues are covered in your divorce settlement.

Your attorney should have your best interests in mind when negotiating your divorce settlement.

Contrary to popular belief, one does not necessarily need an attorney to obtain a divorce. In California, there is such a thing as a summary dissolution, or a "fast-track divorce." According to Deborah Perkins, a family law attorney with a practice in Thousand Oaks, California, the following criteria need to be met in order to obtain a summary dissolution in California:

- The length of the marriage is five years or less.
- There are no children together (born or adopted).
- Debts are below a certain threshold.
- Plus there may be a few other requirements, which varies by state.

Check your state's specific requirements to see if you qualify.

If you don't meet the requirements above, don't despair. Even if you can't afford to retain the services of a family law attorney, there are other options, such as mediation or hiring a consulting attorney.

"Ask your prospective attorney if he or she offers this cost-effective alternative," says Perkins. "It may turn out that you may just need a few hours of the attorney's time to get most of your questions answered. Just prepare well beforehand in order to use this session well."

CHILD SUPPORT

Filing a claim for child support is something you can do for free without an attorney. Often, lawyers won't tell you this, so if money is a factor, look up your state's Department of Child Support Services (DCSS), locate your local office and sign up for their services. The agency will use a set formula to figure the amount of child support due, and they will help you receive that support, sometimes garnishing the wages of a delinquent parent.

> *Filing a claim for child support is something you can do for free without an attorney.*

AUTO INSURANCE POLICY

I wanted to start fresh and take my ex out of our shared auto insurance policy as well. So I called AAA to do that, but I was told that I couldn't. He was the primary insured party. The rep suggested calling him to ask his permission. I didn't want to, I told AAA. I was told e-mail also works, so the rep e-mailed him. He responded after a few days. The end result was that I lost the "marriage discount." Oh well. At that point, I was willing to do almost anything to have everything in my name and in my name alone.

> *Get your own insurance policies post-divorce, including auto.*

You have to consider things like that. Did your lawyer or mediator ever tell you that the auto insurance policy had to be canceled as well? Make that #127 on your post-divorce or breakup to-do list. If you don't cancel your auto insurance, and he's the primary insured, then you can't make any changes. Enough said.

Get your own insurance policies post-divorce, including auto. Who would have thought?

CREDIT CARDS

> *"Always have your own separate credit cards
> and bank accounts. It is fine to have a joint
> account also, but a woman should always
> have access to her own separate money."*

—T. G., VENTURA, CALIFORNIA

I still don't have all the answers to this. The world of credit cards almost seems like a foreign language, akin to learning Swahili or Creole. There's so much fine print and vague jargon. It is similar to treading murky waters. Enough of the metaphors. I'm sure you get my point.

By the time we divorced, we had canceled all the credit cards in his name. He was living overseas anyway. I also wanted to make sure he would stop spending and that I wouldn't get blindsided by a surprise credit card bill.

He agreed that he was responsible for the remaining credit cards in my name. What we failed to do was iron out a payment plan and schedule. Biggest mistake ever. He assumed it was part of his monthly child-support payments. When his earnings started declining, I was stuck with the minimum monthly payments, and my ex was having a sudden attack of debt amnesia.

To this day, I can't get a straight answer from finance experts and lawyers. Should all credit cards be closed? Just joint ones? What if he was using yours or vice versa?

Bruce McClary, vice president for public relations and external affairs of the National Federation for Credit Counseling (NFCC), weighs in on this thorny issue. He says, "First, check your credit history. Then identify the individual and joint accounts and try to arrive at an agreement as to who's responsible for what."

Contrary to popular belief, McClary says it is not necessary to close all joint accounts, as this can negatively impact or sabotage credit scores. You can either remove yourself or the other person in order to keep the account active, especially if it's one that has an extensive credit history, say, a credit card you opened in college.

"Keep the lines of communication open during the early stages of the breakup. Stay positive and productive by establishing and agreeing who's responsible for which credit cards or debts," he says.

McClary also advises women to keep good documentation. "The more records, the better. E-mail is best so you have a record of your discussions and agreements. You'll have something to go back to later," he says.

Don't take no for an answer. I can't stress this enough. I've lost count of the number of times the door was shut in my face or someone hung up on me, saying he or she could no longer help. Call it sheer bullheadedness, but I persisted until I got the answers I needed.

Don't take no for an answer.

Case in point: A financial adviser referred by a close friend was adamant that the only way out of my situation was to do a short sale on the house. My gut told me otherwise. I love my house—so many memories, both good and bad—so I kept asking around and bugging our mortgage lender. Long story short, my mortgage lender agreed to renegotiate my interest rate to a very affordable 1%! I wouldn't have gotten that had I not pestered the bank, right? So who's laughing all the way to the bank? Me!

Oh, and did I mention that we also had a second mortgage? My ex conveniently failed to mention this as he was getting on that flight. Wait. I take that back. He did. But up to the day he left American soil, he maintains it wasn't supposed to be a second mortgage. Anyway, I digress. I will not bore you with those details.

But because our first-mortgage interest rate was slashed, our second-mortgage lender decided to follow suit and also reduced our interest rate. Yes, this is a true story. I can't take all the credit, but it was also as a result of my stubbornness and incessant follow-up phone calls. They just took pity on me. Ha! No. Of course not.

Bank Accounts

You're going to need a checking/savings account in your name at a bank or credit union. If your current bank or credit union works for you, keep it there. But know you have choices. Shop around, and compare rates and fees. Asking friends for advice and searching online should be included in your research.

You'll find that some banks or credit unions offer free checking/savings accounts, whereas others charge a monthly service fee to hold your money for you. Spending some time doing a little comparison shopping can add up to big savings, not to mention satisfaction. Why pay for an account when you don't have to?

Let's face it, especially when you're single—I'll be the first to admit—overdrafts happen. We're waiting for that late check or had to make an unexpected purchase (your son's transportation fee for the track team or when the car battery dies), and, boom, the funds are depleted and beyond, racking up overdraft charges, which can vary among banks/CUs. For example, my big bank charges $34 per overdraft, while my credit union charges $24.

Spending some time doing a little comparison shopping can add up to big savings, not to mention satisfaction. Why pay for an account when you don't have to?

As rates and fees change, you should check into it for yourself. You can check bankrate.com to find the best rates on checking and savings accounts.

Just remember that you have options, and choosing the financial institution that offers the best rates and the lowest fees is definitely in your best interest.

STUDENT LOANS

Sandra, a single mom of two teens, has her master's degree and works as a substitute teacher. Despite her working daily at a healthy pay grade, her budget is tight while raising two kids. Her monthly budget doesn't allow for student loan payments, and like millions of others out there, her loans went into default. While her lenders weren't garnishing her wages, she did lose out on a hefty tax refund every year because of her delinquent loans.

Speaking from my own experience with defaulted student loans, I told Sandra to check into loan-rehabilitation programs. Every lender offers options if paying your loan becomes difficult. These options include hardship deferment, income-contingent payment plans and loan-forgiveness programs. All it takes is a little time and research. Start out by opening the envelopes (I'm sure many of us can relate to piling up the unopened statements we know we can't pay) and calling the number on the loan statement ASAP. The representative will gladly help you and explain all of your options.

Every lender offers options if paying your loan becomes difficult.

It was a happy day celebrating with Sandra this year when she received her tax return, having called her lender, filled out some paperwork and put her loans in a deferred-payment program. She's no longer in default, and her credit will reflect this change in status too. Cheers!

4

MAKING DECISIONS

It is not the creation of wealth that is wrong but the love of money for its own sake.

—MARGARET THATCHER

"I didn't have a whole lot of decisions to make since my life in this area is set. One of the things that I had to do was offload all the 'extras'——the non-income-generating properties like a weekend home in Maryland. I laid a few people off at the office so that I can start cutting costs in the business. I cut down on personal and business expenses that were considered frivolous."

—JENINE D., HARRISBURG, PENNSYLVANIA

WITH EVERY LIFE change, certain decisions have to be made. Being suddenly single again is no exception.

"What I don't want women to think is that they're stuck," says Shirley Kauffman, PhD, a licensed marriage and family therapist in Agoura Hills, California. "There are a lot of options post-breakup."

Kauffman's primary advice after ensuring the woman's safety is to "get the practical things in order" first. Ask yourself these questions:

- Where will you live?
- Do you have enough cash to live on?
- Do you have credit cards to close?

"What I don't want women to think is that they're stuck," says Shirley Kauffman, PhD.

Some decisions to be made are also based on the ages of children involved, says Kauffman. For women with young, school-aged children, it is important to "get it together." You don't necessarily need to tell them everything. The basics will do, such as where Dad is, why you're moving or not, and so forth. Get the children to school every day. Arrange for childcare. Ask family members to come and visit or stay for a while. For those with older children, you can just keep your relationship going, but you can be more honest, she said. You can choose to tell them what happened in whatever level of detail is appropriate.

HOUSING

This is probably the biggest expense and, thus, one of the most important issues for the suddenly single woman, especially those with minor-aged children.

If at all possible, and to keep things as "normal" as can be, staying in your house seems to be the best option. Try to make this part of your divorce/separation agreement. However, if you find yourself drowning in debt in order to remain in the house, consider some creative alternatives such as renting out a room or two.

First, figure out how much extra space you have—one room, two rooms, or more. Can your children share a room if they aren't sharing yet?

Second, assess your comfort level. Are you comfortable being in your pajamas with a stranger? Will you give that person kitchen privileges? If you're in an apartment, is there extra parking available?

Third, get the word out. After making the decision to rent out a room in my house, I posted on Craigslist first. I was cautiously optimistic. Several friends have had a lot of success finding or selling stuff on Craigslist. But, boy, did I get a lot of crazy, creepy responses—from those trying to haggle to pet lovers to men insisting they can be as good as female roommates. My ad said, "Fixed rent, no pets, females only." I guess no one reads anymore.

I did eventually find roommates through word of mouth. If you're like me and you work from home a lot, you might prefer a student or a roommate who works during the day. There is nothing good about the feeling that they are in your space all day long. I treat my renters like family members. They have access to everything in my house, from olive oil to the ottoman. I just ask that they return things to where they belong or replace them if they're depleted. Life has been easy for me on the roommate front.

As house sharing is often more economical than funding an entire household on your own, it is an attractive option for suddenly singles. The key is to find the right person(s) to share it with. Craigslist is one option for advertising rooms for rent; however, if you're looking to be more selective in your roommate search, you may want to look at other options.

CoAbode (coabode.com) is an organization for single mothers looking to share a home. It lists both moms looking for a home and moms who have a home but need a roommate. The shared factor of single motherhood provides a point of relating right off the bat, and roommates often become a source of support in other ways as well, such as sharing childcare or emotional understanding.

Other resources for finding a roommate include college housing boards, where you can list your room for rent. Many colleges have graduate students or students in language programs who may be a little older and more mature than the average college student. And who knows? You may even find a willing babysitter in your (starving?) college-student roomie.

Once you locate a potential roommate, you'll want to be sure to cover a checklist of basics for coexisting.

As with so many things, ask around among friends and family who may know of somebody looking for a place to live. This referral may relieve some of the hesitation you may feel in renting to a total stranger. At least if the potential roommate knows someone who knows you, you can be pretty sure he or she is an upright, safe person to welcome into your home.

On that note, we would recommend doing a background check on any potential roommate just to put your mind at ease. It's inexpensive and worth it. You can go online and find several services that offer background checks for a reasonable fee.

Once you locate a potential roommate, you'll want to be sure to cover a checklist of basics for coexisting, as well as asking him or her what his or her most important concerns are.

I started off moving into a house with another single mother. We connected on Craigslist and met in person at a local coffee shop to see how we got along. After a short meeting during which we (silently) approved of each other's looks, we briefly discussed our situations and budgets. We went to visit the rental house together and walked through, deciding who would get which rooms and for how much. Then we signed the lease and moved in.

All in all, it was a great situation, but there were issues I hadn't thought about before making the move that I now realize are very important. We've come up with a checklist of questions and issues to discuss based on what we've learned (you can find it in the Appendix).

Things like boyfriends spending the night, dishes in the sink and who cleans what and when are issues that should be discussed and agreed upon before moving in together in order to avoid deal breakers and keep conflicts to a minimum. And while you're sure to run into unforeseen issues, if you establish good communication from the start, chances are that you can calmly discuss and resolve any issues that arise.

My first roommate moved out after almost a year to move in with her boyfriend, and I was left to fill the empty room (and pay the extra rent). Interviewing several Craigslist candidates (including one lady who wanted the entire garage for her

Bentley and a man who recounted how his last three roommates had died in accidents and/or from illness) proved interesting, and I finally found a single acquaintance with a small dog (and no deposit) to move in. Each roommate taught me something new about living with others, including knowing exactly what I could and couldn't live with. Our Questions for Potential Housemates (see Resources) encompasses lessons learned through years of experience, the best teacher.

Checking credit is another good idea, although don't let that be your sole decision maker. Despite bad credit, people still need a home, so give them a chance. References from current or past roommates and/or landlords, as well as employers, may provide a more accurate indication of the potential housemate's qualifications. Ask for contact information, and make it a point to contact the references.

OTHER OPTIONS

If you can't keep (or don't have) a house and find yourself having to move, consider resources such as low-income housing in your area (do an Internet search to find them) or housing programs such as Section 8 (HUD). Every county has a local housing authority (search "area housing authority" online to find one in your area), which lists available programs as well as housing options in your location.

Some suddenly singles have decided to live with their exes for a while before making a big change and moving out, which most of us eventually decide to do.

Tina from Ventura, California, is one example. She allowed her ex to remain in the house as a renter, a move which didn't work out as well as she had hoped. Neither could afford the place on his or her own, so to save money and help each other out, they lived as roommates and split rent and utilities. Unfortunately, when her ex lost his job, she also lost out on rent money that she depended on.

In retrospect, says Tina, "I would have kicked him out of the house instead of allowing him to be my renter because once he lost his job, he didn't pay rent for almost a year, and by then, I didn't have the heart to kick him out. So had I just kicked him out when the divorce was final, I would have had rental income. It would have been better to have a clean break."

MAKE IT OFFICIAL

If you do remain in your home, be sure to take your ex-partner's name off of the mortgage or lease to protect yourself.

In my case, I was the one who moved from our shared apartment; however, I didn't think to notify the landlord and take my name off of the lease. Not long after I had moved to California, I received a letter (which found me through my forwarded mail) from my former landlords asking for delinquent rent. They had apparently not received rent for more than a month by the time I received the letter, and they were ready to take legal action.

I contacted them and explained the situation, and, fortunately, they took pity on me and decided not to pursue me for the rent due. They did evict him, though; thankfully, I do not also have an eviction on my record.

My experience is your lesson, however, to remember to take your name off the lease if you move from a rental and your ex decides to stay. And at the very least, notify the landlord of the change to protect yourself from any liability.

Remember to take your name off the lease if you move from a rental and your ex decides to stay.

Caroline, a middle-aged, young-at-heart, now-single woman in Thousand Oaks, feels lucky looking back on the vulnerable position she'd left herself in by moving out of the home she and her husband had shared without taking her name off the mortgage.

"Fortunately, our divorce was amicable, so I didn't take all the precautions I should have," says Caroline. "I was still on his house mortgage, which could have been dangerous had he decided not to pay it."

RELOCATING

In my case, relocating was my best option, although I didn't want to leave my home and everything that was familiar to me. Weighing the pros and cons, however, I decided that family support and a clean break were in all of our best interests.

Starting fresh in a new place is a choice many new singles decide to make. Meredith, a nurse/midwife, doesn't regret her move from California to North Carolina and starting over after her five-year marriage fell apart.

"There is something to be said for liberating yourself from the material possessions and letting go of all the emotional baggage that comes with your house. While I do miss it—that was, after all, my dream house—I know that there will be another home down the road that I will love just as much," muses Meredith. "I have since moved on and learned to love another town and find that security in another space."

Starting fresh in a new place is a choice many new singles decide to make.

CHILDREN

> *"On the last page of our divorce settlement,*
> *it said that the state will not be mediating*
> *regarding child support since my daughter*
> *was not residing in the United States at that*
> *time. I wish that I had made a provision that*
> *my daughter would still receive child support*
> *once she started living here, which was about*
> *five years after the divorce took effect."*

—*M. A. KUCHHERZKI, SOUTH SAN FRANCISCO,*
CALIFORNIA

In addition to the child-support and visitation agreements that you will make, with the help of your legal expert, of course, it's important to have a written directive for the care of your children should you become seriously injured or even die. No, we don't like to think or talk about such a situation, much less actually plan for it.

However, if for some reason beyond your control (and we all know how hard it is to lose that control), you can't take care of your children, the next best thing would be to choose who gets to take care of them.

Talk to your financial planner about writing a living will and trust. This will ensure that your wishes are known and followed whatever the circumstances.

Appointing a guardian is preferable to having your kids swept into the state foster system or having a relative you don't approve of end up raising your children.

Talk to your financial planner about writing a living will and trust. This will ensure that your wishes are known and followed whatever the circumstances.

HEALTH CARE

> *"I didn't feel that there was enough infor-*
> *mation regarding health care. I really had*
> *no clue what to expect, and with all of the*
> *financial issues constantly on my mind, I am*
> *embarrassed to admit that I never thought*
> *about health insurance."*

—*MICHELLE Z., NEWBURY PARK, CALIFORNIA*

When my ex-husband left, I had to purchase health insurance for myself and the kids. It was not cheap, but it wasn't prohibitive either. I know that some women can elect to stay on their ex-spouse's health insurance for a limited amount of time before they need to get it on their own. Check with your ex how long your coverage is expected to last so that you have plenty of time to shop around.

With the advent of the Affordable Care Act (ACA), we qualified for lower-cost health insurance. It's not perfect coverage. Which health insurance is anyway? For one, it does not include dental and vision insurance, which we had gotten used to when my ex was still gainfully employed.

As of this writing, 14 states have set up their own marketplace, including California (CoveredCA.org), New York, Indiana and Washington. If your state is not included among the 14, you can go directly to HealthCare.gov to sign up or enroll for health insurance.

The process of signing up through CoveredCA.org was also not as tedious as I had expected. The paperwork I had to present (most recent paystub or 1099s, in my case) was minimal, and the phone agents were patient and helpful.

Signed into law in 2010, Obamacare, otherwise known as the Patient Protection and Affordable Care Act (PPACA), or Affordable Care Act (ACA) for short, "increases the quality, availability and affordability of private and public health insurance to over 44 million uninsured Americans," according to ObamacareFacts.com.

This year's open enrollment ended on February 15, but certain individuals may qualify for special enrollment if they experienced life events such as marriage, the birth of a child, etc.

Also, don't fret if you and your children qualify under different health plans. Due to the complex income thresholds, you may qualify for Kaiser Permanente's Silver Plan, for example, but your children will be under Medi-Cal or Gold Coast Health Plan.

For me, the important thing was health care coverage, which translates to unquantifiable peace of mind that most single women can relate to.

Vehicles

This is usually a pretty easy one to figure out. Ideally, each of you owns his or her own car and walks away from the partnership with it. However, unraveling intertwined finances can be tricky, especially when both of your names are on legal contracts like car loans. Every situation is unique, but as a general rule, it's often best to refinance your car loan so that each of you is liable for his or her own car. In some cases, you may agree that it makes more sense to pay off the car loan, especially if qualifying for the loan on your own may be questionable or cause your interest rate to increase.

> *As a general rule, it's often best to refinance your car loan so that each of you is liable for his or her own car.*

Look at the numbers, and attempt to arrive at an amicable agreement. If that can't happen, talk to your divorce attorney about the best way to handle the car loan. You may decide to sell off extra cars, trucks, campers, and other large mobile-type toys or determine their value and agree to split them up in a way that makes sense to both of you.

I can't help but revisit my good friend Deena's car lesson here. Deena's husband had recently bought a friend's SUV and given it to Deena as a birthday present. She was thrilled and never thought twice about who owned the car on record. One day soon after she and her husband of 18 years decided to call it splitsville, she was surprised to wake up one day and find that her car wasn't in the driveway. Calling the police, she soon learned the gory details.

Her ex-husband held the pink slip for the SUV, which was also registered and insured in his name. She found herself carless when the police told her the car officially belonged to her husband, leaving her with no legal stake in it. As in the marriage, her ex retained the control by keeping everything in his name. After a week of being carless (try it with three kids!), Deena was able to buy an inexpensive, used minivan to drive around but which often found her stranded on the side of the road in need of another repair.

Couples should have both names on their cars, or each should be the legal owner on record for his or her own car.

I can't stress enough how important it is to have a legal, written record showing that you own your car or property. Couples should have both names on their cars, or each should be the legal owner on record for his or her own car. Spread the word, ladies. Let's protect our sisters, mothers, friends, aunts, nieces, grandmothers, and cousins by empowering them with information about these crucial details.

PETS

When it comes to our beloved creatures, deciding who gets the dog, cat, bird, fish, turtle, or horse often comes down to logistics. The one with the bigger yard keeps the dog, that kind of thing. Of course, sometimes it's obvious who keeps which pet based on a special affinity that makes that pet definitely belong to one of you.

I ended one long-term relationship with my college boyfriend (before kids), with whom I owned two birds—an African Grey parrot and a Scarlet Macaw. We naturally knew which bird went with each of us as we had each bonded more with one of them. (I took Odie, the grey.) Parting with our animal pals doesn't always go smoothly, though, and you may find visitation agreements to their benefit.

One suggestion going forward is if you and a partner acquire a pet, consider getting two so that you each get one in case of a split. (But can you actually split up the animals if you part ways?) Time will tell. I never claimed to have all the answers. Maybe the bigger lesson is to carefully consider your relationship before choosing to raise animals (including children!) together.

5

Managing Bills

It's not how much money you make but how much money you keep, how hard it works for you, and how many generations you keep it for.

—Robert Kiyosaki

O NE SUDDENLY SINGLE woman we know opted to walk away with nothing, "not the house, not furniture, not retirement or pension—and both waived alimony," but managed their joint responsibility (their daughter) while maintaining equality and independence.

"Rather than child support, we kept open our one joint checking account, and we made that our daughter's account. Since custody is 50-50, we both fund the account equally. This account covers our daughter's specific expenses, such as clothes, parties, school, camps, activities, etc. Food, utilities and costs of basic living fall to us both individually for the weeks we have her."

Amicable arrangements like this are a godsend, but not everyone is heaven sent. Single parents especially often feel the brunt of supporting a household singlehandedly, and finances are a main source of stress for too many suddenly singles, as we all know. Psychologist Shirley Kauffman suggests talking it out with a friend, a therapist or in group therapy.

Single parents especially often feel the brunt of supporting a household singlehandedly, and finances are a main source of stress for too many suddenly singles, as we all know.

"A good therapist can help you organize your thoughts and help you come up with a plan regarding finances, bills and all those important matters that need your immediate attention," says Kauffman. "Talking it out with someone can really help."

Deciding to see a therapist is not necessarily going to cost you an arm and a leg. Look into low-cost or free programs in your community. In our area, for example, we are close to a private university which has an on-campus counseling center staffed by licensed therapists and trainees completing their required hours of training. They offer a sliding-fee scale based on income. The only catch is you have to consent for your counseling session to be videotaped sometimes, so it can be used as a training and feedback tool for the trainees.

Group therapy is another less expensive option. Type in "group therapy" and see what options are available in your area.

Shaving Monthly Expenses

If your income changes, look into financial programs offered by utility companies for low-income households. The California Alternate Rates for Energy (CARE) and the Family Electric Rate Assistance (FERA) programs through SoCal Edison, for example, can mean significant savings off your electric bill. The CARE program is also in place at The Gas Company and may lower your gas bill up to 20%. Low-Income Rate Assistance (LIRA) through the California Water Co. can also reduce your water bill.

Ask your utility companies if they have these programs available by calling or going online. The income eligibility guidelines are usually posted on the utility company's website.

Cutting expensive cable and cell phone bills to the lower-tiered, less expensive options is another good idea to leave you with more dollars in your pocket each month. There is increasing evidence that more and more households these days seem to be cutting their cable subscriptions and opting to go with streaming services, such as Netflix or Hulu, for under $10/month.

If you're among the declining number of people that still has a landline at home, consider giving it up, unless you absolutely need it for a fax machine, for example. Even the fax machine is heading towards the path of near extinction. Some are also attached to their landlines because they have seniors living at home, for emergency purposes. Point taken, but the landline is also something to consider cutting.

If you're like us with teens and pre-teens at home, a huge chunk of your income probably goes toward feeding these perennially hungry youngsters. We'll share a few tricks, which you may or may not know by now, like never going to the store hungry. Have you ever done that? Driving home from sports practice, and you realize you don't have dinner covered, so you stop by the store meaning to just grab something quick like a rotisserie chicken and walk out with $90 worth of food you don't necessarily need, just because you're famished? Who needs capers and that tapenade anyway?

Another trick that works for us is menu planning. By Saturday or Sunday, we'll sit down and decide on the following week's meals and cook three to four meals by Sunday afternoon. So practices or not, we have dinner covered and all we need to do is reheat. We eliminate the temptation to eat out or make impulse purchases at the grocery store. I'm sure you have your own tricks to shaving a chunk off of your grocery bill, and we'd love to hear about them. Share the tricks that work for you on our Facebook page: SuddenlySingleForWomen.

Sharing monthly expenses is also one of the benefits of sharing a residence. If you can find someone compatible to share a house with, you can lower your monthly rent or mortgage, and still live in a nice neighborhood. You can also split utility bills and even groceries, if you're a good match. This is something to consider when you're single.

In closing, many finance whizzes repeatedly advise making that annual or semi-annual "check-up" phone call to utility companies, cell phone companies and any provider you pay a monthly subscription to, to see if they have new promos or specials. We knew Geico was on to something with its famous tagline: "15 minutes could save you 15% or more."

These companies usually service millions of households and may not always tell you that the data plan you have been subscribing to is now being offered at $10 less. Ask, ask and ask. Put it on your calendar and schedule these "check-up" phone calls once, twice a year or whatever suits your schedule. Too busy to be put on hold? Put them on speaker while you're reheating dinner or waiting at soccer practice. Enough said.

6

JUGGLING JOBS

She stood in the storm, and when
the wind did not blow her away, she
adjusted her sails.

—ELIZABETH EDWARDS

She believed she could, so she did.

—UNKNOWN

I F YOU'RE LIKE me—someone whose career took a backseat while raising children—you're screwed. Just kidding! It will take a while, though, to get your career back on track, depending on how much time off you took and the demand for your skills.

As a lifelong writer, I've never actually given up the pen or the plume. It was always in the background. Even as a restaurant manager when I was a newlywed, I helped our publicist craft event press releases. I edited and proofread menus, wrote training manuals and job descriptions, and wrote endless business correspondence.

When my ex was in grad school, I helped with finances by transcribing interviews for other grad students. So there were jobs, but there weren't very many. You just have to keep looking and sometimes step out of your job comfort zone.

I knew other spouses then who were underemployed with impressive MAs, MBAs, and PhDs, and yet they were working as receptionists, clerks, and servers. There just weren't many jobs in that East Coast town where we were for two years. Everyone I knew just tried to make the most out of the situation. Did I say the winters were nasty?

I also volunteered like it was no one's business. I helped out in my son's classroom, chaired fundraisers, stepped up to be PTA treasurer, and even volunteered to write grant proposals.

The last one morphed into a paid two-year gig with the school district until funding dried up.

So when my ex walked out the door, my skills weren't completely obsolete, nor did I have zero contacts with the outside world. But it did take time to get back into the game. I am sure I am not the first woman to tell you that her career took a backseat to a man's.

Yes, I've tried it all. Babysitting, check. Admin work, check. Event coordination, check. Blogging, check. Transcribing, check. Selling stuff on eBay, check. Proctoring tests, check. I feel no shame in saying that I do what I have to do when I have bills to pay and children to raise. Call it the lioness syndrome, doing whatever it takes to protect the cubs.

Hopefully, the myriad part-time jobs will only be a transition or a step toward something more permanent. You'll never know, right? But if you are fearless and willing to try anything to make ends meet, there is a job for you out there to fit your schedule, even with kids.

Ride sharing. If you have a newer car, say 2004 or even later, you can check out ride-sharing platforms like Uber, Lyft, or SideCar if they are in your area. It will also help if you have a clean or almost clean driving record. The hours are flexible, and the extra income plus tips (not always to be expected, though) is very helpful. You can drive when the kids are in school, or after work if you have a 9-5 job, or on weekends, when the demand is especially high in certain areas. Think concert venues, stadiums, football arenas, street festivals and other festivities where there's alcohol involved and people don't want to drive home. You set the schedule yourself and drive whenever you want to.

Delivery jobs. Though not as flexible schedule-wise as ride sharing, it is an easy enough job, delivering anything from flowers to fish. Again, the extra money is wonderful. And again, you probably need a clean or almost clean driving record for insurance purposes. Your potential employer will check this, and the insurance underwriters will recommend (or not) whether it's cost effective to add you to their insurance policy based on your driving record.

Babysitting. Like ride sharing, there's some flexibility in looking after other people's children. "As long as you have a house and it's clean, you can probably watch children," says Michelle Z., who watches the children of friends Monday to Friday and makes some decent money doing so. You can set your own schedule—say, you'll only watch children after school or only on certain days of the week. Of course, your earning potential is higher if you do it full time or almost full time. The only downside is being stuck in the house all day and not having much adult interaction. The latter can be remedied by walks to nearby parks, playgrounds, and other gathering places, provided the little ones are cooperative.

Craigslist. I know I said the roommate ad thing did not work out for me here, but I did get a short-term project through this popular, free site. I advertised my services (writing, editing, proofreading, blogging, and administrative work) and landed a five-month gig assisting a busy entrepreneur with various local businesses and organizing his office. You might still get some crazy queries, but legitimate and lucrative jobs of all types can be found here.

Freelance sites. Thumbtack is one of the great sites out there on the Internet where you can find freelance work. Whatever service you provide, be it writing and editing, babysitting, dog walking, house cleaning, painting, car repair, or what have you, Thumbtack provides a forum for finding customers who want your service. The Internet abounds with sites like this, and many are specialized to specific industries. Elance is a site to find projects from writing and editing to computer programming and illustrating. Taskrabbit specializes in domestic help and party planning. Search online for "freelance job sites." New sites seem to appear daily.

Academic exchange. Several opportunities to earn extra dollars exist in the field of academic exchange. High school students looking to spend a year in the United States need host families every year, and many international student-exchange programs, such as the Program of Academic Exchange (PAX), offer commissions to local community coordinators to locate host families and provide support for the duration of the program. Educational Foundation (EF) is another. Again, an Internet search will yield a list of programs you can sign up to represent and earn a commission without spending all of your time working. This is especially great if you are involved and connected with the community.

Recycling. Sometimes we overlook the simple things like recycling. My family and I have a separate container next to the trash for recyclable items such as glass, aluminum, and plastic. When the container is full, I take it to the local recycling station and trade it in for cash. While you probably can't support yourself by recycling (though some people do, judging by the loads of recycling they bring in), recycling is an easy way to turn your trash into cash. Every little bit helps, right? Super industrious singles may explore the idea of making money by collecting their neighbors' and friends' recycling, especially if they don't recycle on their own. Adding a few others' recycling to yours starts adding up to some serious change.

7

Reinventing Yourself

If plan A fails, remember there are
25 more letters.

—Chris Guillebeau

NETWORKING

Before you tell us that there is no networking in the playground or in a mommy-and-me class, we'll point out that the mom sitting next to you, pushing her toddler on the swing, is the CEO of a Fortune 500 company or that the mother of the child your son is now playing with is a publishing bigwig you've been hoping to meet. As I'm sure most of you have found out by now, many women have had careers BMK (before marriage and kids) and still maintain them on a part-time or superwoman basis.

There are also phone apps like MeetUp.com. I have the app on my phone, and I've used it to find business networking and social groups, from hiking to horticulture. You can get alerts as well as reminders if there are group meetings near your zip code.

Many women have had careers BMK (before marriage and kids).

If you have a business, check out your local chamber of commerce too.

CLASSES

> *"Get educated. It is the best thing you can do*
> *for yourself, whether you are still married or*
> *not. No one wanted to hire me, even for a pizza*
> *delivery job, because my skills were outdated."*

> —BELINDA LAROSA (NOT HER REAL NAME),
> THOUSAND OAKS, CALIFORNIA

Just like taking part-time jobs, you have to be willing to go back to school and brush up on your skills, though a college degree is probably not a must for everyone or for all careers.

I did sign up for Spanish classes. It's almost the law in California, where every other want ad asks for bilingual applicants. I also took basic accounting classes and signed up for writing workshops to brush up on my skills.

You never know who you're going to run into for a job lead or a referral.

Check out the local adult school if there's one near you. The one nearest my house has classes ranging from astrology to app building and from cooking to comedy writing. It's also a good excuse to get out there and network. You never know who you're going to run into for a job lead or a referral.

SUPPORT GROUPS

*"For those days when you feel like hiding,
mascara and lip gloss make a world of difference—and a long, hot shower really soothes
all the anxieties and worries. For those sleep-
less nights, just keep watching your breath."*

—*LENN M., NEW YORK, NEW YORK*

Know that you're not alone. Thousands of women have walked
this path, and while it may be the first time you're going through
this experience, help is out there. Sometimes women are reluc-
tant to ask for help, but reaching out for support is nothing to
be ashamed of. Abundant resources exist for women in transition. You can find helpful resources such as support groups and
various organizations by asking a friend or family member or
searching online in your area.

**Thousands of women have walked this path, and
while it may be the first time you're going through
this experience, help is out there.**

Focusing on the positive, overcoming challenges and gaining strength and courage from others in similar situations are
tools that were key to Peggy Jacquez's journey during her personal transition. Peggy shared her story as part of the "Women

Who Inspire" series sponsored by GIFT (Gaining Insight for Transition), a program for women founded by Sepideh Yeoh, a school-board member who was inspired to help women in transition. "I'm hoping to create opportunities for women in transition," says Yeoh, whose monthly speaker series features women who have been through transition and have valuable insight and lessons to share. In addition, small support groups allow women to connect with others and address specific needs such as parenting, financial and work issues.

In addition to sharing her personal story, Peggy, an account executive at America's Job Center of CA, offered practical information about free employment services provided by America's Job Center of CA and the Workforce Investment Act.

Such examples of other women's success can inspire others to more easily navigate their own challenging paths.

SOCIAL CIRCLES

"Post-divorce and [as] part of my New Year's resolutions, I promised myself that I would go out of my way to meet new people—not to date or to meet men but to make new friends. There are so many interesting people out there, but sometimes we isolate ourselves when we're deep into our misery."

—S. K., NEWBURY PARK, CALIFORNIA

If you're like me, along with in-laws, you probably have lost some friends deliberately or accidentally. A friend of mine calls this phenomenon "the divorce fallout."

When you and your ex decided to go your separate ways, I'm sure some friends found themselves at a crossroads. His friends probably went with him, not that they have any ill feelings toward you but as part of a natural progression of their friendship with him. Your friends probably did the same.

"Don't isolate yourself," says Kauffman. "Make an effort to meet new people, whether it's through your church, your gym, a hobby or a new class."

So it's time to make some new friends or reconnect with old ones that might have been neglected during your relationship or marriage. I joined a local hiking group and made some new friends there. I also started volunteering with my daughter at a homeless shelter. I embraced some newfound friendships and basked in the novelty of it. Here were new people who don't know my history or are not tired of hearing me vent about my ex. I embraced the new company, knowing that they are not whispering behind my back or thinking about the telenovela that is my life.

PHYSICAL FITNESS

The experts are right. The natural high we experience from an endorphin rush post-exercise is a good antidote to stress and sadness.

The hiking group I recently joined not only provided me with companionship on the trails, but the group kept me fit and also provided me with support without their knowing it. It was "me" time. Just mine. Expectations were low fitness-wise and conversation-wise. I kept to myself when I needed to and chimed in when I had something to contribute. There was no pace we needed to keep. I took my time some days and hung out with some ladies in the back. There have also been good days when I was in the lead pack.

Joining a new group was therapeutic for me. This new group knew nothing about me or my ex. There was no "So how is he doing these days?" or "Have you collected back child support yet?" It was refreshing to start on a clean slate.

Spirituality

"I was already very spiritual before my marriage unraveled. But I feel like it has even helped get me through the most difficult times."

—S. K., Newbury Park, California

Yoga has been my go-to exercise for years, and I find myself resisting or not finding the time for it and becoming more and more stressed. When I finally take the time for yoga—and stillness, breathing, and stretching—I am incredibly refreshed and rejuvenated afterward.

Meditation, walking in nature and listening to music are other forms of spiritually relaxing, unwinding activities.

Of course, so is going to an organized church service of any kind. Whatever it is that renews you and allows you to take time out of the daily grind and appreciate your life and the connection we have to others and the divine, make time for it. We all know the benefits, and we need them. Making the effort to pursue these spiritual interests is essential to a happy, fulfilled existence.

8

Moving Forward

I want to do it because I want to do it.
Women must try to do things as men
have tried. When they fail, their failure
must be but a challenge to others.

—Amelia Earhart

"I had to put my energy on rebuilding rather than on recovering what was lost."

—*JENINE D., HARRISBURG, PENNSYLVANIA*

PEOPLE MOVE FORWARD in many different ways at various rates of speed. While there is no set time or range, Kauffman believes the average woman usually takes anywhere from two to five years to recover emotionally from the ordeal of a breakup. But there is no set timeline as there are many variables and factors to consider.

A woman who got left holding the bag with credit card debts and back taxes will probably take a longer time to heal due to anger and resentment issues with her ex. I know; I've been there. Someone who didn't have that many entanglements holding her back may be able to move on faster.

The presence of children may also delay the healing process, especially when there are issues that need to be dealt with regarding their care, visitation, schools, child support, and so forth.

Domestic violence is also another factor to consider. When there are physical as well as emotional scars, the healing process may be prolonged.

Setting or Reevaluating Goals

> *"It happened post-long-term-relationship breakup. I realized I couldn't rely on the expectation of marriage to take care of myself. That year I made five goals: new, great, better-paying job; buy (own) house; get master's; new relationship/get married; and have a child. I did all except the master's part and only because I'm terrified of debt. It was the best thing that ever happened to me, learning late-onset financial and emotional independence."*

> —S. S., Hamilton, Virginia

Working with a life coach or career counselor is a great idea. Experts can teach you what you don't already know, and another person can provide you with different ideas about or perspectives on your situation. Knowing all of your options and clarifying your priorities can help you formulate the best plan for your life.

Find a mentor in your field. That person will not automatically knock on your door or land in your lap. You have to find that person. Say that you're an aspiring financial adviser; you will most probably be assigned a trainer or a mentor while you're in the process of getting licensed. Absorb as much as you can about the industry. Don't be bashful about asking questions. If the trainer assigned to you is too busy, pick the brains of someone else. Attend as many classes as you can. Soak up online resources. Set goals by asking what the next level up is and what you need to do to reach that level.

If you're a writer or editor like us, align yourself with someone whose work you admire. Offer to co-write or research an important story for free. Tag along on reporting assignments. Attend workshops; there are lots of free ones out there. Expand your repertoire. If you've been writing features since time immemorial, try another beat—food, sports, or travel. Study various writing styles. Better yet, study your editor's writing style. If you work at a publication, find out what you can do to get more assignments or how to move up to assistant editor.

Saving and Investing

> *"My husband died even before he was 40. He had a $25,000 life insurance policy but no pension or anything. We had five young children, a mortgage, and bills to pay, but, thankfully, I also had a full-time job at the local phone company. I kept working until my children were all out of the house. I invested in real estate and turned them into rental properties. I was a big saver, too, and had a lot of family nearby to help with everything from groceries to after-school care."*

> —Mary M., Newbury Park, California

So how do you start saving if you're in the hole? Little by little and pay yourself first. It could be as little as $10 a week or $100 a month. Just start somewhere, and don't feel bad if you can't do it consistently.

Saving a little at a time is better than not saving anything at all. Don't beat yourself up if you fall behind or if you have to borrow from those savings for emergencies. Just get back up on the savings wagon.

"There is risk of not taking action," says another financial planner we met. "Losing money." The sooner you start saving money can mean the difference between thousands and millions in savings.

PUTTING YOURSELF FIRST

"I miss my old outgoing, life-loving self, and I want to get that old me back as soon as I put this behind me."

—S. K., NEWBURY PARK, CALIFORNIA

"You decide what road you want to take. You have a lot of choices, and you can change your mind even after you have made a choice," says Kauffman.

Almost everyone says it's quicker to heal emotionally than financially. Agreed. The emotional pain goes away over time, but the financial effects tend to linger. I mean really linger.

If your credit is shot, it will take some time to repair it. If your ex took out loans or maxed out your credit cards like mine did, it will also take more than a few years to dig yourself out of that financial hole.

But don't despair. Think Helen Reddy (for those of us old enough to remember her words of wisdom): "Yes, I'm wise, but it's wisdom born of pain. Yes, I've paid the price, but look how much I've gained. If I had to, I can do anything…I am strong… I am invincible. I am woman!" For a real boost, listen to and watch the song on YouTube. And remember that you can rebuild your credit one step at a time.

9

Resources

If you look at what you have in life,
you'll always have more. If you look at
what you don't have in life, you'll never
have enough.

—Oprah Winfrey

SUDDENLY SINGLE COMMUNITY

Suddenly Single Facebook page
http://www.facebook.com/SuddenlySingleforWomen

Universal Love Foundation (providing tools and assistance to single-parent families)
http://www.universallovefoundation.org

Group Therapy
http://groups.psychologytoday.com/

The National Foundation for Credit Counseling
https://www.nfcc.org/index.php

Federal Trade Commission
https://www.consumer.ftc.gov/articles/0153-choosing-credit-counselor

A People's Choice (legal-document assistant service)
http://www.apeopleschoice.com/california-family-law/california-divorce/divorce-requirements-in-california

Legal Zoom (online legal-document help)
http://www.legalzoom.com

Suze Orman (personal finance guru)
http://www.suzeorman.com

America's Job Center of California
http://americasjobcenter.ca.gov/

FINANCIAL INFORMATION AND EDUCATION

womeninvesting.net

marketwatch.com

money.cnn.com

SuzeOrman.com

dailyworth.com

askLizWeston.com

wealthysinglemommy.com

mydollarplan.com

Financial Planners

MerrillEdge.com
TransAmerica.com
Vanguard.com
UBS.com

Appendix A:

Questions You Need to Ask

O UR LISTS OF questions can also be found on our Suddenly Single for Women Facebook page, where you can download a PDF version to print and bring along with you to your interviews.

Questions for Family Law Attorneys

Interview Questions for Family Law Attorneys
How long have you been an attorney?
How many divorce cases have you handled?
Why did you decide to become a divorce attorney?
Do you represent either women or men most often?
What makes you a better divorce lawyer than the one down the street?

What is the time frame for this divorce? Six months? One year?

What steps are involved? What happens during the steps?

How much does it cost? How is it billed? Monthly? Up front?

Are your fees average, low, or high compared to those of other divorce attorneys?

Who pays court costs?

Do you recommend mediation in some cases? If so, when?

Do you recommend legal clinics?

What are the advantages of hiring an attorney to handle my divorce?

How many other divorce cases do you handle at once? Do you have enough time for mine?

Is it important that an attorney work in my local county courts regularly?

Have you gone through a divorce? (personal but maybe)

QUESTIONS AFTER YOU'VE CHOSEN YOUR FAMILY LAW ATTORNEY

What are my rights as a woman in this state?

What's the first step after I hire you (gather paperwork, show up in court, etc.)?

What paperwork do I need to give you?

What's the best way to divide assets?

Am I responsible for paying any debts? Do we divide debts as well as assets?

How is child visitation determined?

What if any of our agreements are broken? Is there any penalty for that, or do we just go back to court?

What are the most common mistakes you see people (especially women) make during their divorce proceeding?

Should I sell my house?

QUESTIONS FOR POTENTIAL HOUSEMATES

Here are some questions you'll want to ask (in no particular order) as you're interviewing potential housemates:

Can you afford the rent?

Do you need to be reminded about paying the rent? How (verbal, e-mail, text)?

Do you work? Where? For how long?

Are you normally home during the day, at night, or on weekends?

Have you ever been evicted?

Are you a neat person?

Are you planning to have overnight guests?

Do you entertain often?

Do you smoke, drink, or do drugs?

Do you have kids? If yes, what are their ages, and how often will they be living with you?

Do you have pets? What types (indoor/outdoor, etc.)?

Do you have any allergies that would require me to keep certain foods out of the house?

Do you have any special needs I should know about?

What are your needs or concerns regarding lifestyle or sharing a home?

How many vehicles do you have?

Do you have any crazy, unpredictable exes who might come looking for you?

How often do you clean house or your room and bathroom?

Do you wash dishes after a meal or let them sit for a while?

Do you have your own appliances (refrigerator, microwave, etc.)?

Do you have your own dishes, silverware, cups, pots and pans, and so forth?

Do you play loud music? What type of music do you like?

Are you a night owl or an early bird?

Are you a quiet or loud person?

How do you resolve conflict?

How would you describe your personality?

Do you like a lot of communication?

Have you ever been arrested? If so, for what?

Do you have any history of violence?

Do you cook?

Do you want to share food or cook separately?

How do you want to divide up the housework?

Do you have furniture you'll want to bring over other than what's in your room?

Do you need storage or use of the garage?

Do you need space in the pantry or cabinets?

Appendix B: Financial First Aid Kit

(Adapted from The Wall Street

Journal and Bankrate.com)

S OME RECOMMENDED DOCUMENTS you need to have in place before an emergency or unforeseen event hits you:

Health

Emergency contacts
Medication and supplements list
Health information and history
Medical power of attorney
Durable power of attorney in case of incapacity
Living will
Health insurance information
Organ donation information

Banking and Investments

Bank accounts
Investment accounts
Annuities
Retirement accounts
Safe deposit box
Important financial contacts

Insurance

Life insurance
Long-term care insurance (if separate from life insurance)
Additional policies

Estate

Durable power of attorney
Will
Estate plan
Funeral arrangements and related information

Other Important Information

Websites and passwords
Memberships and subscriptions
Credit cards
Copies of marriage license, titles to vehicles, deeds to house/
other properties, forms of IDs

MISCELLANEOUS
Dependents and guardianships
Loans
Partnerships
Unfulfilled responsibilities

Appendix C: Glossary

401(k) Plan

A qualified plan established by employers to which eligible employees may make contributions on a post-tax and/or pretax basis. Employers offering a 401(k) plan may make matching or non-elective contributions to the plan on behalf of eligible employees and may also add a profit-sharing feature to the plan. Earnings accrue on a tax-deferred basis.

403(b) Plan

A retirement plan for certain employees of public schools, tax-exempt organizations, and certain ministers. Also known as a tax-sheltered annuity (TSA) plan.

Alimony

Sometimes called spousal support, designed to provide financial support to the lower-income spouse, over and above child support.

Annuity

A contractual financial product sold by financial institutions designed to accept and grow funds from an individual. Upon annuitization, it pays out a stream of payments to the individual.

Capital Gain

A profit from the sale of a property or investment.

Child Support

Court-ordered payments, typically made by a noncustodial divorced parent, to support minor children.

Cosigner

Other than the principal borrower, a person who signs for a loan. The cosigner assumes equal liability for the loan. Having a cosigner is a way for individuals with a low income or poor/limited credit history to obtain or get approved for a loan.

Credit Report

A detailed report of one's entire credit history, which includes personal data, a credit history, and details of accounts. The three big credit bureaus (Experian, TransUnion and Equifax) provide it for free once a year through AnnualCreditReport.com.

CREDIT SCORE

A number assigned to a person that indicates to lenders that person's capacity to repay a loan. Generated by Fair Isaac Co., or FICO, this three-digit number is now showing up for free on some credit card statements.

DIVIDEND

A distribution of a portion of a company's earnings, decided by the board of directors, to a class of its shareholders. Dividends can be issued as cash payments or as shares of stock or other property.

DIVORCE

The legal dissolution of a marriage by a court or other competent body.

FIXED INTEREST RATE

The interest rate charged on the loan will remain fixed for that loan's entire term, no matter what market interest rates do. This will result in payments being the same over the entire term.

FORM 1099-MISC

A tax form that reports the year-end summary of all nonemployee compensation. It covers rent, royalties, self-employment and independent-contractor income, crop-insurance proceeds and various kinds of miscellaneous income.

FREELANCER

Also known as an independent worker, a contractor or someone self-employed; people such as writers and editors who are not committed to a particular employer long term.

LEASE

A legal document outlining the terms under which one party (lessee or renter) agrees to rent property from another party (lessor or property owner). The lessee makes regular payments to the lessor for a specified number of months or years. Both parties must uphold the terms of the contract for the lease to remain valid.

LEGAL SEPARATION

A circumstantial divorce without a legal decree, it usually entails a court order that two spouses can live apart as unmarried persons, except that they are still married. A couple that is legally separated must still deal with the typical divorce-related issues such as alimony, child support, child custody, and property division.

MEDIATOR

A person who attempts to make people involved in a conflict come to an agreement; increasingly used in divorces, a neutral third party who helps both parties negotiate an acceptable divorce agreement.

PERMANENT LIFE INSURANCE

An umbrella term for life-insurance plans that do not expire (unlike term life insurance) and combine a death benefit with a savings portion. This savings portion can build a cash value against which the policy owner can borrow funds or withdraw the cash value to help meet future goals such as paying for a child's college education. The two main types of permanent life insurance are whole and universal life insurance policies.

POSTNUPTIAL AGREEMENT

A contract created by spouses after entering into marriage that outlines the ownership of financial assets in the event of a divorce. The contract can also set out the responsibilities surrounding any children or other obligations for the duration of the marriage. Also known as a post-marital agreement or post-nup.

Prenuptial Agreement

A type of contract created by two people before entering into marriage. This contract could outline each party's responsibilities and property rights for the duration of the marriage or upon dissolution of the marriage. Also known as a pre-nup.

Principal

The amount borrowed or the amount still owed on a loan, separate from interest.

Restraining Order

A temporary court order issued to prohibit an individual from carrying out a particular action, such as approaching or contacting a specified person.

Roth IRA

The Roth IRA is a retirement savings account to which individuals can make contributions with after-tax dollars. If certain requirements are met, distributions from the Roth IRA will be tax-free.

Rule of 72

A finance rule that involves dividing the interest rate by 72 to determine the amount of time it takes to double your money.

SUMMARY DISSOLUTION

A simpler, quicker way to end a marriage or domestic partnership in California without a court appearance. Certain requirements must be met.

TERM LIFE INSURANCE

A policy with a set duration limit on the coverage period. Once the policy is expired, it is up to the policy owner to decide whether to renew the term life insurance policy or to let the coverage end.

TRADITIONAL IRA

An individual retirement account (IRA) that allows individuals to direct pretax income, up to specific annual limits, toward investments that can grow tax deferred (no capital gains or dividend income is taxed). Contributions may be tax deductible depending on the taxpayer's income, tax-filing status and other factors.

VARIABLE-INTEREST RATE

On a loan, the interest rate charged on the outstanding balance varies as market interest rates change. As a result, payments will also vary (as long as payments are blended with principal and interest).

Further Reading

Don't Worry, Retire Happy, **by Tom Hegna**

T HIS BOOK IS for anyone interested in retiring worry-free. A mathematical, scientific formula applied to your specific situation (single, divorced, married) shows you how to maximize your Social Security benefits. What you don't know can lose you money! I found this book on a KCET special, so you know it's good, solid material. Hegna impressed me by explaining how following his retirement planning tips allowed a 57-year-old newly divorced woman who had not saved enough money for retirement to retire comfortably!

Smart Women Finish Rich, **by David Bach**

A how-to guide on controlling one's financial future and finishing rich. Includes a nine-step plan for spending wisely and aligning money with one's values.

The Automatic Millionaire, **by David Bach**

Includes an easy approach to financial security and making your financial life automatic even as you sleep.

Start Late and Finish Rich, **by David Bach**
Outlines an easy-to-follow catch-up plan for savings procras-tinators or for those who just got sidetracked by unexpected challenges.

Women & Money: Owning the Power to Control Your Destiny, **by Suze Orman**
A groundbreaking book on women overcoming challenges, get-ting rid of the things that hold us back, and changing the way we think about our finances.

Suze Orman's Financial Guidebook, **by Suze Orman**
Comparable to having a one-on-one financial planning session with Suze; full of self-tests and questions.

Comeback Moms, **by Monica Samuels and J. C. Conklin**
Good reading for women who are ready to leave the workforce, with tips on how to reenter with a bang.

Rich Dad, Poor Dad: What the Rich Teach Their Kids about Money That the Poor and Middle Class Do Not!, **by Robert Kiyosaki**
A tale of two dads and their differing philosophies on money and investing.

27331815R00091

Made in the USA
Middletown, DE
15 December 2015